Aspects of English Sentence Stress

Aspects of English Sentence Stress

BY SUSAN F. SCHMERLING

University of Texas Press, Austin & London

Library of Congress Cataloging in Publication Data

Schmerling, Susan F   1946-
  Aspects of English sentence stress.

  A revision of the author's thesis, University of
Illinois at Urbana-Champaign, 1973.
  Bibliography: p.
  1. English language—Accents and accentuation.
2. English language—Grammar, Generative. I. Title.
PE1139.S33 1976   425   76-6561
ISBN 0-292-70312-0

Copyright © 1976 by University of Texas Press

Printed in the United States of America

TO MICHAEL

Contents

Acknowledgments

This book is a modest revision of my 1973 University of Illinois dissertation, which was written during my first year of teaching at the University of Texas at Austin. I am enormously indebted to a large number of people at both institutions for stimulating discussions, examples, feedback on early drafts, and general encouragement, and I thank all of you; special thanks are due Lee Baker, Arlene Berman, Dwight Bolinger, Wallace Chafe, Peter Cole, Georgia Green, Chuck Kisseberth, Jerry Morgan, and Michael Szamosi. I must also express my gratitude to Bob King for encouraging me to publish this revision, and to the University of Texas Press, a nice publisher to work with.

Aspects of English Sentence Stress

Introduction

Despite differences in approach and interest, linguists working in the theoretical framework which now dominates American linguistics—the framework which is generally referred to as *generative grammar*—have accepted as a fundamental goal of linguistics the formulation of an explicit theory of the ability of the native speaker of a language to pair sounds and meanings. Theoretical disputes aside, linguists have in common that they are blessed (or cursed, depending on how one looks at it) with an inability to take for granted the remarkable fact that every "normal" child—every child not suffering from some gross physical, mental, or social handicap (e.g., deafness, severe retardation, isolation from other human beings)—is able, on the basis of a finite amount of data, to construct a system of rules which enable him to produce and understand an infinite number of novel utterances. A model of the linguistic competence which the child acquires is thus a desideratum of all linguists working in this framework.

As has long been recognized, however, the relationship between the pronunciation of an utterance and its meaning is not a direct one. To engage in some oversimplification, linguists have recognized three aspects of utterances in natural language: their pronunciation, their meaning, and their "form." Consequently, linguists have come to speak of three subfields of linguistics which correspond to these aspects of utterances: phonology, semantics, and syntax. A complete model of a speaker's linguistic competence must thus include not only a model of these three aspects of utterances but also a theory of how they are related.

It was not until the middle 1960's that the goal of formulating a model of the relationships between these aspects of utterances was realized, and the model which emerged—the model associated with Chomsky's *Aspects of the Theory of Syntax* (1965), or so-called *Aspects* model—answered questions concerning the specifications of these relationships in the following fashion: an adequate model of syntax alone had to recognize more than one "level" of representation of an utterance, a conclusion arrived at earlier by Chomsky in *Syntactic Structures* (1957). Furthermore, among the various syntactic representations of an utterance, two could be singled out as having special significance. One syntactic representation of an utterance was directly related to its "meaning" by a system of "semantic projection rules," such as that outlined in Katz and Fodor 1963 and Katz and Postal 1964, while the other was directly related to a "phonetic representation" by a system of phonological rules which was worked out most fully in Chomsky and Halle 1968. These two significant levels of representation were referred to as the *deep structure* and the *surface structure*, respectively, of an utterance. Thus, in the *Aspects* framework, a grammar consisted of three components. The syntactic component was the "creative," or *generative*, component of the grammar; the semantic and phonological components *interpreted* the structures generated by the syntactic component by assigning them a meaning and a pronunciation respectively. The *Aspects* model thus embodied two crucial empirical claims concerning the relationships among these three linguistic aspects of utterances: that there was *one* syntactic level of representation of an utterance that was directly related to its meaning, and that there was *one* syntactic level of representation—a distinct one—directly related to its pronunciation. Neither of these claims has gone unchallenged, though more attention by far has been focused on the first than on the second.

It is generally accepted today that the first of these claims is false—that there can be no level of deep structure in the *Aspects* sense. The question which is debated today is not whether such a level exists, but whether a distinction between "syntactic rules" and "semantic interpretation rules" (in the sense used above) can be maintained, and whether a significant "syntactic" level of representation exists which is distinct from semantic representation, surface structure, and perhaps "shallow structure." Ironically, in view of the relatively recent arrival of semantics as a legitimate subfield of linguistics proper, comparatively little attention has been given to the question of the relationship between syntax and phonology—that is, the question of whether a level of surface structure in the *Aspects* sense can be defined.

The lack of attention given to this latter question is all the more ironic in view of the fact that several serious challenges have appeared in the literature to the view that there is an "interpretive" phonological component—that syntactic rules (and semantic interpretation rules, if the distinction between the two is maintained) require no phonological information and that syntactic information at *one* level of representation can be required by phonological rules. Bierwisch (1968) and Pope (1971), for example, have argued that certain prosodic rules require access to information not present in an independently motivated surface structure, while Baker (1971) argues for the existence of a syntactic rule which requires prosodic information. A different sort of problem has been noted by Bierwisch (1966) and Chomsky and Halle (1968): cases where intonation breaks fail to coincide with the major constituent breaks one would expect in a "syntactically motivated" surface structure. These linguists have thus argued for "readjustment rules" which would alter constituent structure. It is interesting to note the assumptions that seem to underlie the discussion of the need for a "readjustment component" in Chomsky and Halle 1968. One is that rules which have the effect of altering constituent structure may be divided into two classes, those which are "syntactically motivated" and those which are "phonologically motivated," and that those rules belonging to the latter class can all be ordered after those belonging to the first. The second is that the existence of a definable level of surface structure no longer has the status of an empirical claim.[1]

The significance of the challenges to the existence of an "interpretive" phonological component extends beyond the fact that they are serious and the fact that they have been largely ignored. One feature which all these challenges have in common is that they relate to a specific aspect of pronunciation: prosodic properties of utterances. It would thus appear that a prerequisite to the formulation of a more adequate theory of the relationships between phonological and other aspects of utterances is a greater understanding of such prosodic properties. This book is a modest attempt in that direction. It deals with one prosodic aspect of utterances, that which is usually referred to as sentence stress.

The study of stress presented here is not a phonetic study; it is a study of what might be called the syntax of stress. That is, I am concerned here not with the phonetic nature of stress but with the ques-

tion of "which stress goes where": the abstract principles which appear to be involved in assigning relative prominence to the different
items in an utterance. I am thus defining stress for the purposes of
this study as *subjective impression of prominence*,[2] and I leave open
questions concerning the phonetic nature of this prominence. There
is an important reason for doing this beyond the fact that I am not a
phonetician: as phoneticians have long been aware, a precise characterization of the articulatory and acoustic correlates of the subjective
impression of prominence usually referred to as stress is elusive.
There seems today to be general agreement among phoneticians
working in this area that stress cannot be characterized along any one
physical parameter and particularly that intensity or "loudness"
plays a relatively minor role in such prominence, traditional defini-
tions of stress notwithstanding.[3] One can conclude that, to the extent that it is necessary to refer to stress as an entity, this entity must
be considered to have a psychological rather than a simple physical
reality. While the value of experimental studies of this entity is in no
way denied here, it thus seems to be the case that the question of
what linguistic entities are needed in a representation of stress in an
utterance will be answered only when we have an idea of what entities we need to talk about in formulating the principles involved in
stress assignment. It is thus my hope that the principles which are
presented informally in this book will help contribute to an understanding of what stress "is."

Because I am taking no stand on the physical nature of stress, no
theoretical significance should be attached to the notation I use in
the examples, which was chosen purely for convenience. To assist the
reader in interpreting the examples, however, a brief discussion of
this notation is in order. Except in my discussion of the Chomsky-
Halle treatment of stress, I will be using more-or-less standard stress
diacritics. The acute accent (´) is used to indicate the heaviest stress
in a sentence (or phrase). The circumflex (^) is used in two ways
here. When it precedes a ´, it indicates a heavy stress which is only
slightly less prominent than a ´; I would thus indicate the citation
pronunciation of my name as *Sûsan Schmérling*. As indicated in
Chapter 5, I believe the difference between ^ and ´ in this example
to be a quite low-level one, and I take no stand here on the question

of whether it is proper to view this difference as one of stress per se or one of intonation. When the circumflex is used following a ´, it indicates a significantly lower "level" of stress; thus I use it in a representation of the most nearly "neutral" pronunciation of *There's a cár cômíng*. This use of the circumflex is a bow to Trager-Smith tradition; I do not, however, intend a claim that a ´ˆ contour contrasts with a ´ˋ contour, a contrast whose existence is somewhat controversial (see Vanderslice and Ladefoged 1972). A grave accent (ˋ) is used preceding a ´ to indicate a stress level which is significantly lower than ´, that is, lower by a degree which is more significant than the degree to which ˆ differs from a following ´. Finally, a breve (˘) is used to indicate items which I have found it convenient to view as not being assigned stress (see Ch. 4). I have thus found no necessity for distinguishing more than these four "levels" of prominence, and, in fact, I am dubious about any significant phonetic difference between what I have marked with ˘ and what I have marked with ˋ. (It should be noted, however, that I have here ignored the "reduced stress" frequently found on certain auxiliaries, conjunctions, and so forth, for which the ˘ is perhaps more traditionally employed.) In my discussion of Chomsky and Halle's treatment of stress I will for purposes of consistent page appearance follow their practice of using superscript numerals, with the convention that 1 = ´, 2 = ˆ, and 3 = ˋ.

This book is organized into six chapters. This first discusses the approach to sentence stress of Chomsky and Halle 1968 and that of two earlier works, Newman 1946 and Trager and Smith 1951. Following a review of the different approaches and the claims made by the various authors, a detailed critique of the cyclic treatment of Chomsky and Halle is presented, in which it is shown that such a treatment is unmotivated and beset with serious difficulties. Chapter 2 is a review and critique of more recent approaches to sentence stress by Joan Bresnan and George Lakoff and a third approach, by Dwight Bolinger, which, while not new, has only recently become widely known to generative grammarians. Chapter 3 is a discussion of a concept which has received little serious discussion but has been extremely important in discussions not only of stress itself but also of syntax, the concept of "normal stress." It is shown in this chapter that this notion is one which is incapable of characterization in any linguistically significant way and thus that treatments of stress (and other phenomena) which depend on it are without empirical basis. The "positive" chapters of this book are Chapter 4, where the question of what items in an utterance are assigned stress is discussed, and Chapter 5, which deals with relative stress levels. Chapter 6 contains a summary and a methodological moral.

It is the thesis of this work that sentence stress assignment is governed by several different principles of different natures. The statement of these principles is for the most part beyond the scope of current linguistic theory. Consideration of sentence-stress phenomena indicates, then, that it is impossible to view all rules governing pronunciation as belonging to an "interpretive" component of the grammar. The relationship between the pronunciation of a sentence and other properties is as complex, and as deserving of respect, as the relationship between the meaning of a sentence and other properties, and we are still very far from having an adequate theory of linguistic competence.

1 The Cyclic Approach

One of the fundamental claims of generative grammar is that the phonological component of the grammar "interprets" surface structures—the "output" of the syntactic component—by assigning them a pronunciation. While most of the work done in this framework concerning the phonological component of the grammar of English has been concerned with word-level phonology, the above claim is intended to include *all* aspects of pronunciation, and it can reasonably be said that there is a "received" analysis of English sentence stress, namely, that outlined by Chomsky and Halle in *The Sound Pattern of English* (1968, henceforth *SPE*). Chomsky and Halle's claim is that sentence stress is (almost) entirely predictable from the stress of individual words and the hierarchical organization of the utterance at the level of the input to the phonology (which, on their account, may differ from surface structure in certain respects specified by rules belonging to a "readjustment component"). Their claim is quite explicit:

> Once the speaker has selected a sentence with a particular syntactic structure and certain lexical items . . . the choice of stress contour is not a matter subject to further independent decision. That is, he need not make a choice among various "stress phonemes" or select one or another "superfix." With marginal exceptions, the choice of these is as completely determined as, for example, the degree of aspiration. Similarly, a hearer who has grasped the structure and morphemic constitution of an utterance from a rough sampling of the physical input need not attend to stress variation, to whatever extent that may actually be a physical property of utterances. (*SPE*, pp. 25–26)

Beyond the level of word stress, Chomsky and Halle account for the placement of sentence stress by two rules: the Compound Rule (CR) and the Nuclear Stress Rule (NSR). Stated informally, the CR assigns primary stress to the leftmost primary-stressed vowel in a noun, verb, or adjective, while the NSR assigns primary stress to the rightmost primary-stressed vowel in a major constituent (stress being treated as a feature of vowels). These rules apply according to the principle of the transformational cycle, outlined as follows in *SPE*:

(a) The rules of the phonological component are linearly ordered in a sequence $R_1, \ldots, R_n$.
(b) Each rule applies to a maximal string containing no internal brackets.
(c) After applying the rule R_n, we proceed to the rule R_1.
(d) Unless an application of R_n intervenes, the rule R_j cannot be applied after the rule R_i ($j < i$) has applied.
(e) R_n is the rule: erase innermost brackets. (*SPE*, p. 20)

By a general convention on the application of stress-assignment rules, whenever a rule assigns primary stress, all other stresses within the domain of application of that rule are lowered by one. The stress-lowering convention thus permits the ultimate assignment of an indefinitely large number of stress levels by rules which are formulated to assign primary stress.

Because of its limited relevance to the topic under discussion here, I will ignore the CR in what follows and concentrate on the NSR.[1] We can illustrate the application of this rule by a simple-minded example, *Jóhn hìt Bìll*:[2]

$$(1) \; [_S[_{NP}John]_{NP} \; [_{VP}[_V hit]_V \; [_{NP}Bill]_{NP}]_{VP}]_S$$

1	1	1	Word stress
	2	1	NSR
2	3	1	NSR

The [231] stress contour of this sentence is thus attributed by Chomsky and Halle to two facts: (*a*) *John*, *hit*, and *Bill* are all items which can be assigned primary stress by word-stress rules, and (*b*) the sentence is represented in its "phonological representation" as having a right-branching constituent structure. Two aspects of surface structure are therefore critical to the assignment of stress in this analysis: the category membership of the individual items involved and the constituent structure of the utterance.

Thus, beyond the level of the word, the NSR is intended to account for all "normal" stress contours. The assignment of non-"normal" contours is presumably to be effected by some other rule(s); Chomsky and Halle say nothing about this matter beyond the comment, "We assume that the position of emphatic stress is marked in the surface structure, and we neglect matters that we have assigned to the theory of performance" (*SPE*, p. 25, n. 13). *Emphatic stress* is not defined here, and Chomsky and Halle do not specify what sorts of stress phenomena they would assign to the theory of performance.

Chomsky and Halle consider an extremely limited amount of evidence concerning sentence stress in *SPE*; the treatment outlined there seems to be essentially a translation into a generative framework of Chomsky, Halle, and Lukoff 1956. This earlier work develops a system of rules for assigning phonetic stress levels to phonemic transcriptions in which only the opposition stressed/unstressed is marked, on the basis of a similar cyclic principle using a hierarchical arrangement of junctures.[3] In their paper, Chomsky, Halle, and Lukoff were not concerned with the discovery of new data concerning sentence stress; they were, rather, reinterpreting data which were well known at the time, data presented in Newman 1946 and Trager and Smith 1951. It may therefore be instructive to examine the claims made in these latter works.

Newman's insightful and still influential article was not a study of sentence stress per se but a phonemic analysis of English stress in which he set up three stress phonemes, each having two allophones. While his observation of a contrast between *I have instrúctions to leàve* 'I'm to leave instructions' and *I have instrúctions to léave* 'I've been instructed to leave' (using Newman's notation for stress) is the best-known contribution of this article today, it was Newman's treatment of his heavy stress phoneme which had the greatest influence on work related to sentence stress in the late 1940's and 1950's. In *SPE* (p. 90), Chomsky and Halle cite the following claim of Newman's in support of the NSR: "When no expressive accents disturb a sequence of heavy stresses, the last heavy stress in an intonational unit takes the nuclear heavy stress (Newman 1946:176)." They thus appear to interpret Newman's claim in such a way that *heavy stress* is equivalent to *primary stress assigned by a previous rule application* and that *intonational unit* is equivalent to *major syntactic constituent*. If their interpretation is correct, then, Newman would be claiming the same thing Chomsky and Halle are claiming with their NSR: that the rightmost element in any major syntactic constituent will bear the greatest stress in that constituent, provided that it is an item that can be assigned primary stress by a word-stress rule (which, on Chomsky and Halle's account, is equivalent to saying that it must be a member of a "stressable" syntactic category).

A careful reading of Newman's analysis reveals, however, that his claims differ from those of Chomsky and Halle in two important ways. In claiming that the rightmost "heavy stress" in an "intonational unit" was heavier than the others, Newman was not claiming that the rightmost word in such a unit would necessarily have a "nuclear heavy stress" (his name for the "louder" allophone of his heavy stress phoneme); he was making the much weaker claim that it would have the nuclear heavy variety of stress *if it bore a stress assigned to the heavy stress phoneme*. This claim leaves open the possibility that the rightmost word in the "intonational unit" might be assigned to some other stress phoneme, and his example *I have instrúctions to lèave* clearly indicates that he was allowing for the possibility that the rightmost word might have other than a heavy stress even if it was a member of a major syntactic category. Newman was clearly limiting his discussion to what he saw as allophonic variation among those stresses which he assigned to his heavy stress phoneme, his claim being that the rightmost such stress would be louder than the others and would bear the melodic contour characteristic of the type of "intonational unit" of which it was the "nucleus." On Chomsky and Halle's account, however, *leave* should be assigned a primary stress in this example by a word-stress rule since it is a member of a category (Verb) to which word-stress rules apply. Thus it should subsequently be a candidate for stressing by the NSR.

The second important respect in which Newman's claim differs from that imputed to him by Chomsky and Halle is in the nature of his "intonational units," which Chomsky and Halle identify with syntactic constituents (or perhaps simply with the domains of stress-rule application, which in their account happen to be syntactic constituents). Though Newman fails to state a definition of *intonational unit*, it is clear from his discussion that he intends a concept similar to what phonologists would today call a *phonological phrase* or a *breath group*. Newman identifies a number of different types of "intonational units" according to the melodic contours he claims are typically associated with each; on the basis of such melodies he identifies *declarative*, *interrogational*, *enumerative*, and *divisional* "intonational units." The following example will illustrate the sort of approach Newman is taking; his notation is used here:

(2) He bróught a cráte of óranges＿﹨twó bárrels of ápples＿﹨ and
    a básket of péaches﹨

On Newman's account, this sentence contains three nuclear heavy stresses (the acute accent indicating all stresses which Newman assigns to his heavy stress phoneme, both nuclear and "subordinate" heavy stresses): on *oranges* and *apples*, which he terms the nuclei of enumerative units, and on *peaches*, the nucleus of a declarative unit. These units are identified by a particular type of rising tone, in the case of the enumerative units, and a falling tone in the case of the declarative unit. It thus seems clear that Newman is defining such units intonationally, not syntactically.

That Newman's approach is significantly different from that of Chomsky and Halle is thus clear in two ways. First, his discussion of examples like (2) makes it clear that he intends his intonational units to be structured *linearly*. They are thus entities of a quite different nature from syntactic constituents, which are structured *hierarchically*. Not only are these units characterized differently from syntactic constituents: it is clear that the two sorts of units cannot be identified with each other. (Note that the "enumerative unit" *he brought a crate of oranges* in example [2] is not a constituent in any syntactic theory.) It should thus be obvious that Newman's principle *is not a cyclic one*. Second, Newman's factual claim concerning what items in an utterance will bear a nuclear heavy stress is a far weaker one than that of Chomsky and Halle. As will be shown below and in Chapter 5, Newman's claim fits the facts concerning English stress far better than theirs.

Trager and Smith's claims, which appear to have had a greater influence on Chomsky, Halle, and Lukoff, differ from Newman's in several respects, many of which appear to follow from differences in their phonemic analysis. Trager and Smith found it necessary to posit *four* stress phonemes; one can for the most part identify Newman's "subordinate heavy stress" with Trager and Smith's "secondary stress." The significant aspect of Trager and Smith's analysis for our purposes here is their attempt to relate stress contours to syntax. On Trager and Smith's account, stress phonemes combine with "+ junctures" to form suprasegmental *morphemes*, which they termed *superfixes*. Their claim was that it was possible to identify certain syntactic constituents by the superfix which these bore. A √ ´ +` superfix (to use their notation), for example, identified a constituent as a noun; note that this claim is echoed in Chomsky and Halle's CR. The claim of Trager and Smith which has the greatest significance for the history of the treatment of sentence stress, however, is their version of the greatest-stress-at-the-end principle, stated as follows:

> . . . the primary stress of a phonemic phrase will come as near the end as possible; here 'as possible' means that some items, such as pronoun objects, certain adverbs, prepositions, and others, do not have primary stress though they are normally the last thing in a phrase, and they get primary stress only with the shift morpheme. (Trager and Smith 1951:75; on their shift morpheme, see Chs. 3 and 4 below.)

Trager and Smith's claim is thus the model for all claims concerning a direct relationship between "stressability" of items and their category membership, and the influence of this claim on Chomsky and Halle should be obvious. Chomsky and Halle have followed Trager and Smith in claiming that the rightmost item in whatever type of unit is being discussed will have the heaviest stress if it is a member of a "stressable" category. This claim is far stronger than Newman's claim concerning the distribution of his nuclear heavy stress, though the difference in claims seems not to have been widely recognized.

Despite the similarity between Trager and Smith's claims and those of Chomsky and Halle, however, there are differences. Trager and Smith's "phonemic phrases" do not have an internal, hierarchical structure and thus differ in this respect from syntactic constituents taken as a class. And, for Trager and Smith, the presence of a final primary stress in a "phonemic phrase" does not entail a necessity that some other specific stress phoneme precede this primary stress. That is, the claim quoted above concerns only the final stress of the superfix; both $\sqrt{\hat{}+'}$ and $\sqrt{`+'}$ superfixes are recognized by Trager and Smith. Because of the cyclical application of the NSR, however, Chomsky and Halle's treatment makes claims not just concerning the final stress of a constituent but concerning entire stress *contours*. While Chomsky and Halle's analysis of sentence stress is based on Newman's and Trager and Smith's data, the claims it makes are stronger than the claims made in either of these earlier works. Chomsky and Halle do not, however, consider any data which would support the stronger claims they are making.

Not only do Chomsky and Halle fail to consider the differences between their own claims and the claims of those on whose data they apparently base their analysis, but very little evidence appears in *SPE* in support of the claims that are made there. That it is the surface structure of an utterance which determines its stress contour is simply taken for granted;[4] Chomsky and Halle state:

> It is well known that English has complex prosodic contours involving many levels of stress and pitch and intricate processes of vowel reduction. It is clear even from a superficial examination that these contours are determined in some manner by the surface structure of the utterance. (*SPE*, p. 15)

The arguments for the principle of the cycle are not much more convincing. Chomsky and Halle follow the statement quoted above by the statement that

> *it is natural to suppose* that in general the phonetic shape of a

> complex unit (a phrase) will be determined by the inherent
> properties of its parts and the manner in which these parts are
> combined, and that similar rules will apply to units of different
> levels of complexity. These observations suggest a general prin-
> ciple for the application of rules of the phonological compo-
> nent, namely, what we shall call the principle of the "transfor-
> mational cycle." (*SPE*, p. 15; emphasis added)

They state further:

> Notice, once again, that the principle of the transformational
> cycle is a very natural one. What it asserts, intuitively, is that
> the form of a complex expression is determined by a fixed set
> of processes that take account of the form of its parts. *This is
> precisely what one would expect* of an interpretive principle
> that applies to phrase markers, in this case, surface structures.
> (*SPE*, p. 20; emphasis added)

The principle of the cycle may indeed be intuitively appealing, but it
does not follow from this that it is correct. Thus, arguments against
it should not be considered especially iconoclastic.

Despite the paucity of evidence adduced in favor of the *SPE* approach, it has generally been assumed that this approach works prop-
erly for simple sentences and that problems arise only in an attempt
to extend it to more complex sentences. In what follows I shall argue
that this approach is misguided even for quite simple phrases and sentences. It should be noted that none of the arguments given below
can be said to prove conclusively that the cyclic approach is wrong.
In each case cited, various ad hoc remedies easily suggest themselves.
Nevertheless, the number of such remedies necessary seriously calls
the psychological reality of the *SPE* approach into question. As
Chomsky and Halle note, a consequence of their claims is the following:

> It is reasonable to suppose that the principle of the transforma-
> tional cycle and the principles of organization of grammar that
> we have formulated in terms of certain notational conventions

are, if correct, a part of universal grammar rather than of the particular grammar of English. Specifically, it is difficult to imagine how such principles could be "learned" or "invented" in some way by each speaker of the language, on the basis of the data available to him. It therefore seems necessary to assume that these principles constitute a part of the schema that serves as a precondition for language acquisition and that determines the general character of what is acquired. While the general principles of organization of a grammar that we have been discussing can most plausibly be regarded as part of universal grammar, it seems that such rules as the Main Stress Rule must, in large part at least, be a part of the particular grammar of English. A reasonable tentative assumption, then, is that the Nuclear Stress Rule, the Compound Rule, and the Main Stress Rule must be learned by the child acquiring the language, whereas the conditions on the form of rules, the principle of the transformational cycle, and the principles of organization embodied in the various notational conventions that we have established are simply a part of the conceptual apparatus that he applies to the data.

The Nuclear Stress Rule, the Compound Rule, and the Main Stress Rule, in its various cases, assign primary stress in certain positions. A very small body of data concerning the position of primary stress in simple utterances is sufficient to justify these rules. Correspondingly, a small body of data of this sort might be sufficient to enable the language learner to postulate that these rules form part of the grammar of the language to which he is exposed. Having accepted these rules, the language learner can now apply the general principles of universal grammar to determine their effects in a wide variety of cases. As we have seen, very simple rules can have extremely complex effects when applied in accordance with these general principles. (*SPE*, pp. 43–44)

Thus, if Chomsky and Halle are correct, the Nuclear Stress Rule *should* be applicable in a great variety of cases. Additional rules which bleed or undo the effects of the NSR, or special conditions on the NSR, should not be necessary, if the NSR has the generality claimed for it. Thus a grammar containing the NSR and a variety of ad hoc remedies certainly violates the spirit, if not the letter, of the *SPE* approach.

The first phenomenon I shall consider in discussing the viability of the NSR is phrases with [231] contours. It will be recalled that, assuming a surface structure like that in (1), the NSR as originally formulated will correctly assign a [231] contour, as indicated. There are, however, many other cases of phrases with [231] stress contours which the NSR cannot account for, such as NPs in which the prenominal constituent must be assigned [21] or [31] stress in isolation. Such examples include complex adjectives:

(3) $\overset{2}{c}$ontext-$\overset{3}{s}$ensitive $\overset{1}{r}$ule (cf. $\overset{2}{c}$ontext-$\overset{1}{s}$ensitive)[5]
(4) $\overset{2}{b}$rand $\overset{3}{n}$ew $\overset{1}{c}$ar (cf. $\overset{2}{b}$rand $\overset{1}{n}$ew)

other types of prenominal phrases:

(5) $\overset{2}{o}$ver-the-$\overset{3}{c}$ounter $\overset{1}{s}$ale (cf. $\overset{2}{o}$ver the $\overset{1}{c}$ounter)
(6) $\overset{2}{M}$onday-$\overset{3}{m}$orning de$\overset{1}{p}$ression (cf. $\overset{2}{M}$onday $\overset{1}{m}$orning)

adjectives with productive prefixes:

(7) $\overset{2}{u}$nkn$\overset{3}{o}$wn $\overset{1}{q}$uantity (cf. $\overset{3}{u}$nkn$\overset{1}{o}$wn)
(8) $\overset{2}{a}$ntic$\overset{3}{o}$mmunist $\overset{1}{s}$peech (cf. $\overset{3}{a}$ntic$\overset{1}{o}$mmunist)

numbers:

(9)   f$\overset{2}{i}$ft$\overset{3}{e}$en $\overset{1}{p}$eople (cf. f$\overset{3}{i}$ft$\overset{1}{e}$en)
(10) th$\overset{2}{i}$rty-f$\overset{3}{o}$ur $\overset{1}{p}$eople (cf. th$\overset{2}{i}$rty-f$\overset{1}{o}$ur)

proper names:

(11) M$\overset{2}{a}$ry $\overset{3}{A}$nn Sm$\overset{1}{i}$th (cf. M$\overset{3}{a}$ry $\overset{1}{A}$nn)

adjectives modified by adverbs:

(12) b$\overset{2}{a}$dly wr$\overset{3}{i}$tten p$\overset{1}{a}$per (cf. b$\overset{2}{a}$dly wr$\overset{1}{i}$tten)

(13) wéll²-óiled³ machíne¹ (cf. wéll²-oíled¹)

and various other cases where the word in prenominal position is not structurally complex, but where stress alternations occur nevertheless:

(14) Rómance²³ lánguage¹ (cf. Rómance³¹)
(15) Víetnam²³ wár¹ (cf. Víetnam³¹)
(16) Chámpaign²³-Urbána¹ (cf. Chámpaign³¹)[6]

Examples of verb phrases displaying this property also exist. These include verb-particle constructions:

(17) lóok² úp³ the ánswer¹ (cf. lóok² it úp¹)
(18) lóok² óver³ thése¹ pápers (cf. lóok² it óver¹)

complex adverbials:

(19) prétty² néarly³ díed¹ (cf. prétty² néarly¹)
(20) was véry² bádly³ dóne¹ (cf. véry² bádly¹)

and, again, productive prefixes:

(21) óverstated²³ his cáse¹ (cf. óverstated³¹)
(22) únderestimated²³ the cóst¹ (cf. únderestimated³¹)

The problem here is that, unlike example (1), which has a right-branching constituent structure, these examples all have left-branching structures.[7] Thus, the NSR will not assign [231] contours but rather [321] contours, as illustrated by the sample derivation in (23):

(23) $[_{NP}[_?[_N\text{context}]_N$ $[_A\text{sensitive}]_A]_?$ $[_N\text{rule}]_N]_{NP}$

1	1	1	Word stress
2	1		NSR
* 3	2	1	NSR

There are, of course, several logically possible solutions to this problem, such as a later patch-up rule. Such a rule might be formulated to switch around the nonprimary stresses in the relevant constituents.[8] However such a rule were formulated, it would have an important negative characteristic: it would not be formulated to assign primary stress. Since much of the attractiveness of the phonological cycle derives from its putative ability to formulate stress-assignment rules which do just that, the existence of such a rule would weaken the foundations of the cycle to a certain extent.

Another way out which might be suggested and must be discarded is the possibility that some readjustment rule(s) would actually alter the constituent structure so that the NSR could yield the correct output directly. Disregarding the ad hoc nature of such a rule and even the question of how such a rule could in fact be formulated, it should be noted that these examples are still phrased with left-branching structure, even though they have [231] stress contours. Compare an example like (17) with the minimally contrasting (24):

(17) look up the answer
(24) look up the flagpole (adverbial reading)

In (17), *look up* is pronounced as a phrase: there is a much greater pause potential between *up* and *the* than between *look* and *up* or *the* and *answer*. In (24), on the other hand, the greatest pause potential is between *look* and *up*. The phonological evidence here correlates with the syntactic evidence: *up the answer* in (17) is not a constituent.

The point of this discussion concerning these phrases is not that the NSR cannot be salvaged, however. The important thing is the existence of the data themselves. Example (1) is a paradigm case of the NSR working as it should: that is, given some independent characterization of normal stress where the [231] contour is correct, the NSR correctly predicts this contour and does so on the basis of constituent structure—the right-branching structure presumably also independently motivated. What the additional examples here suggest is that the correlation between constituent structure and stress contour in (1) may be something of an accident: [231] contours seem to be quite common in English phrases, right-branching *or* left-branching. A grammar containing the NSR thus claims in effect that for these phrases a [231] contour obtains *because of* constituent structure in the right-branching cases and *in spite of* constituent structure in the left-branching cases. I know of no evidence for such a remarkable claim.

A second area which presents serious problems for the cyclic approach to stress concerns sentences with coordinate constituents. Because the NSR as formulated in *SPE* assigns primary stress to the rightmost primary-stressed vowel in any major constituent, it predicts that the rightmost conjunct in a coordinate constituent should receive greater stress than those to the left. This is not in general the case; thus we have

(25) $\overset{2}{\text{Jo}}$hn and $\overset{2}{\text{Bi}}$ll $\overset{3}{\text{hi}}$t $\overset{1}{\text{Ha}}$rry.
(26) $\overset{2}{\text{Jo}}$hn $\overset{3}{\text{wa}}$shed and $\overset{3}{\text{dri}}$ed the $\overset{1}{\text{di}}$shes.

That is, the stress of each of the conjuncts is the same as the stress it would receive in a nonconjoined version. Once again, several ad hoc remedies come to mind; there are various ways one might constrain the NSR so that it would not apply in coordinate constituents. However, not only would such a remedy be thoroughly ad hoc—the cyclic approach claims there is no reason why the NSR should *not* apply in such instances—but it would also be too general, since in sentence-final position the rightmost conjoined constituent does receive greater stress:[9]

(27) Jŏhn hĭt Bĭll and Hárry.

Note, however, that simply permitting the NSR to apply in a sentence-final coordinate constituent will not produce the correct results, either; rather, a [2341] contour will be assigned:

(28)

$[_S[_{NP}John]_{NP} [_{VP}[_V hit]_V [_{NP}[_{NP}Bill]_{NP} and [_{NP}Harry]_{NP}]_{NP}]_{VP}]_S$

	John	hit	Bill	Harry	
	1	1	1	1	Word stress
			2	1	NSR
		2	3	1	NSR
*	2	3	4	1	NSR

Thus some other, postcyclic, rule would be needed to ensure that the rightmost constituent of a sentence-final coordinate constituent would receive greater stress. Such a rule would, of course, duplicate the NSR in an obvious and serious way.

Suppose, on the other hand, that we abandon the principle of the cycle and look for some other explanation for the data. Newman's nuclear heavy stress principle immediately springs to mind as an account of why the stress levels in coordinate constituents should differ only in final position, since, on his account, we would expect to be heavier only that stress which bears the falling declarative intonation contour. Newman's principle will not, of course, explain the contours in the sentences where the cyclic approach really seems to work—sentences with [231] contours like (1)—since it in no way predicts that the verb should be less prominent than the subject. But suppose that some other principle exists which says that *John* and *Bill* in that example should receive greater stress than *hit*. Then Newman's principle (or something very much like it) would explain why

Bill receives greater stress than *John*. As we shall now see, sentences with intransitive verbs, which provide a third problem area for the NSR, provide some support for this possibility.

Since the NSR applies within any major constituent and works by assigning primary stress to the rightmost primary-stressed vowel in a given constituent, it predicts that in a sentence like (29) the primary stress will fall on the verb, with the subject receiving secondary stress:

(29) John died.

There is no question that such a stress contour is possible; it might, for example, be used in a context where the discourse participants know that John has been in critical condition and the speaker is informing them that John did, in fact, die. Note, however, that without this special assumption on the part of the speaker, a [12] contour obtains, as in the following:

(30) Why are you looking so glum? —John$\overset{1}{J}$ohn di$\overset{2}{e}$d.
(31) Oh, my God, I see here that John$\overset{1}{J}$ohn di$\overset{2}{e}$d. That means I'm the only member of the old gang left.

The question one asks at this point, of course, is this: which of these contours is "normal" and therefore to be accounted for by the same principles that account for other instances of "normal" stress? It should be clear that there is no immediately satisfactory answer to this question, which is discussed in detail in Chapter 3. For the moment, however, I shall consider the [12] contour to be "normal," since it is the one involving a minimum of special assumptions.

A sentence like (29) is not an isolated example. Some more examples which fail to receive a final primary stress are these:

(32) I have to go home—my c$\overset{1}{o}$usin's coming.
(33) Hey—your c$\overset{1}{o}$at's on fire!
(34) Watch out—there's a c$\overset{1}{a}$r coming.
(35) Waiter, there's a fl$\overset{1}{y}$ in my soup.

(36) I don't know what I'm going to do—I don't have any
     money and the rént's due.
(37) I'm going out of my mind with all those bélls ringing.
(38) You left the wáter running.
(39) When I got home I realized my wállet was missing.

Notice that the primary stresses in these examples cannot be explained away as being "contrastive" if "contrastive stress" is to be a
notion more meaningful than "nonnormal" stress (see Ch. 4). On the
contrary, if primary stress is placed on the final constituent—where
the NSR would place it—a feeling of "contrast" often *is* conveyed.

It is still not impossible to salvage the NSR here, of course, even if
these contours are considered "normal." All we need do is formulate a new rule to assign primary stress to the subjects of intransitive
verbs and order this rule before the NSR.[10] We would thus be claiming that the stress contours of sentences like these were determined
by principles completely different from those operating in a sentence
like (1) (in addition to begging the question of why the cyclic approach fails again). Notice, however, that these sentences and (1) do
indeed have something in common: the verb receives lower stress
than the subject or direct object; in other words, the predicate receives lower stress than its argument(s). Is this a linguistically significant generalization? The cyclic approach denies that it is. We shall
see in Chapter 5, however, that there are good reasons to suppose
that in sentences like these—simple statement-of-fact sentences,
where the whole sentence is "news"—there is a principle which puts
lower stress on predicates than on their arguments, irrespective of
their linear position in surface structure.

A final area I will discuss which displays difficulties for the cyclic
approach involves adjective-noun sequences. According to the cyclic
approach, the relative stress on adjectives and nouns in noun phrases
should be purely a function of the depth of embedding of the phrase
and its linear position in surface structure. This approach is unable in
principle to explain a contrast like that exemplified by (40) and
(41):

(40) When I went to Europe I saw some un$\overset{2}{u}$sual s$\overset{1}{i}$ghts.
(41) When I went to Europe I saw all the $\overset{3}{u}$sual s$\overset{1}{i}$ghts.

The contrast in stress contours in these examples appears to be related to a difference in the logical structures of these sentences: (40) discusses sights which were unusual, but (41) does not refer to sights which are usual, whatever these might be. These sentences are by no means an isolated pair of examples; (40) patterns with other examples which can plausibly be derived from a reduced relative clause (as in Smith 1964 and other works), such as *r$\overset{2}{e}$d s$\overset{1}{u}$it* and *g$\overset{2}{o}$od b$\overset{1}{o}$ok*, while (41) patterns with other examples where the adjectives have some other source, such as those illustrated in (42)–(44):

(42) The police arrested the wr$\overset{3}{o}$ng m$\overset{1}{a}$n.
(43) Malnutrition is the pr$\overset{3}{o}$bable c$\overset{1}{a}$use.
(44) I'll go look it up in my Fr$\overset{3}{e}$nch gr$\overset{1}{a}$mmar.

Some more contrasts are illustrated in (45)–(48):

(45) This isn't the sort of behavior I'd expect from n$\overset{2}{o}$rmal ch$\overset{1}{i}$ldren.
(46) When I looked in the room I didn't see any of the n$\overset{3}{o}$rmal ch$\overset{1}{i}$ldren.
(47) The text is very good, but page 27 contains a l$\overset{2}{o}$usy f$\overset{1}{o}$ot-note.
(48) The only mention he makes of my work is a l$\overset{3}{o}$usy f$\overset{1}{o}$ot-note!

A probably related contrast occurs with quantifiers, according to whether or not these are under the scope of a negative. If they are, a [31] contour obtains; if they are not, we find a [21] contour:

(49) The target wasn't hit by m$\overset{3}{a}$ny $\overset{1}{a}$rrows.
(50) The target was missed by m$\overset{2}{a}$ny $\overset{1}{a}$rrows.

Notice that, to the extent that paraphrases like *arrows which are many* are good at all, such paraphrases are possible for cases like (50) but not for cases like (49). Given the notoriously vexatious problems involved in the analysis of quantifiers, however, I shall say no more about this matter here.

Still another example of this phenomenon is provided by the following well-known example from Trager and Smith 1951:

(51) Long Island is a long island.

Once again, *l$\overset{2}{o}$ng $\overset{1}{i}$sland* seems to involve a reduced relative clause; *L$\overset{3}{o}$ng $\overset{1}{I}$sland* does not.

Thus, to save the *SPE* approach, an ad hoc remedy would again be needed.[11] Notice, furthermore, that, by the cyclic approach, any NPs with [21] contours should be impossible except in isolation. Chomsky and Halle in fact noticed this problem; they state:

> . . . a simple adjective-noun construction such as *sad plight* will have the contour 21 in isolation, the contour 32 in the context *his —— shocked us*, and the contour 31, with different internal relations, in *consider his ——*. As the structure of the sentence becomes more complex, the internal relations of stress within a phrase of this sort will continually be modified. Thus in the sentence *my friend can't help being shocked at anyone who would fail to consider his sad plight*, the surface structure might indicate that the word *plight* terminates no less than seven phrases to which the Nuclear Stress Rule applies, so that successive applications of this rule would give the contour *s$\overset{8}{a}$d pl$\overset{1}{i}$ght*. Presumably, the actual internal relations of stress in *sad plight* are the same, in this case, as in *consider his sad plight*, or even in *sad plight* in isolation. (*SPE*, p. 23)

Chomsky and Halle seem to consider this a minor difficulty with the cyclic approach.[12]

The problems caused by the indefinite lowering of stress levels permitted by the stress-lowering convention have been noted by other writers as well, most notably Bierwisch, who points out that simply assuming a cutoff point beyond which stresses fail to be lowered predicts that "most of the originally primary stresses in a sufficiently complex sentence will be completely levelled" (1968:175)—a prediction which is clearly false. Chomsky and Halle appear not to take such problems very seriously because of their conviction that stress is almost entirely a psychological rather than a physical reality and that the principle of the cycle is part of our innate linguistic endowment; they thus state explicitly that they view questions concerning the number of stress levels that can be distinguished to be "of little significance." Their view of stress is one they attempt to support with the claim that phoneticians with training in the same conventions are remarkably consistent in the stress levels they assign to utterances of their native language, despite the fact that these "stress levels" do not seem to correspond to any physical reality. If this latter claim were true it would, of course, provide strong evidence for the mentalistic view of stress which Chomsky and Halle profess (though it is not obvious how it provides any support for the cycle specifically), but to the best of my knowledge there is no experimental support for this claim. Indeed, Lieberman (1965) (whom Chomsky and Halle cite in a footnote, implying that he supports their position) found in a series of famous experiments that two linguists who had extensive experience using the Trager-Smith notation for stress and pitch actually *disagreed seriously* in the transcriptions they gave of the same English utterances. Lieberman concluded that the clear-cut distinction between stress and pitch assumed by Trager and Smith simply did not accord with the facts of psychological reality—and their references to stress and pitch indicate that Chomsky and Halle follow Trager and Smith in maintaining this distinction.

As we have seen, there is considerable evidence that the principle of the cycle receives little support from consideration of a number of simple phrases and sentences, and in discussing these cases I tried to grant Chomsky and Halle all of their assumptions. There is, however, a reason for questioning the assumptions that underlie the cyclic approach to stress. A primary motivation for the cyclic approach is the claim that the stress contours assigned smaller units in isolation are "preserved" when these are placed in larger constructions.[13] Thus, those linguists who maintain a cyclic principle assume that word stress is something which is always present—that is, that if word-stress rules assign the greatest stress to a particular syllable of a word, that syllable will always be more prominent than the other syllables in the word, regardless of the position that word occupies in an utterance (unless "contrastive stress" is involved). This factual claim is not new to Chomsky and Halle; it was maintained by Trager and Smith as well. Other linguists, however, such as Pike (1945; 1947) and Bolinger (see especially Bolinger 1958b) have held the view that word stress is a potential thing: saying that some word is stressed on a particular syllable is for them equivalent to saying that *if* that word is stressed in a given utterance, *then* the stress will go on that particular syllable. Bolinger states this view as follows:

> I would say that the word *compost* is stressed on the first syllable; but this would not mean that in any given instance the syllable *com-* was more prominent that the syllable *-post*. Indeed, in an utterance having the pitch profile of the following,
>
> ```
>                        do
>      What did you
>                    with that compost?
> ```
>
> *com-* and *-post* would be about equal in prominence, or lack of it. The pitch prominences, or accents, belong not to individual items but to the utterance, which in this example happens to have conferred one on *do* and none on *compost*. Saying that *compost* is stressed on the first syllable is then to say only that if *compost* receives an accent, the syllable *com-* is the one that will be made prominent by it, as in the following:
>
> ```
>                                    com
>      What          do with that
>           did you                 post?
> ```
>
> —where pitch accents are conferred on *what*, *do*, and *compost*. (1961a; reprinted in Bolinger 1965:123)

Thus, in this view, sentence-stress assignment is something which is logically prior to word-stress assignment—the opposite of the cyclic point of view.

Notice that what is involved here is a dispute over the facts: this should be an empirically testable issue. And, in fact, an observation made by James Sledd at the First Texas Conference (see Hill 1962a) suggests very strongly that the "potential" view of stress is the correct one. Sledd asked:

> . . . why do stress-distinctions that seem perfectly plain under some intonations disappear under others? A *Spánish stúdent*, with high pitch and primary stress on *student*, is quite different from a *Spánish stûdent*, with high pitch and primary stress on *Spanish*. But consider the following sentence [with Trager-Smith pitch levels and junctures indicated]:
>
> $\overset{2}{I}$'m $\overset{31}{\text{going}}$ | $\overset{1}{\text{said}}$ the Spanish $\overset{1}{\text{student}}$ ||
>
> I have tried this sentence over and over on a good many different people, and I never get more than fifty percent accuracy at recognizing either of the items in this frame. (Hill 1962a:36–37)

Sledd, and the others present at the conference, seemed to feel that the stress difference was still there in this case but that it was, for some reason, "hard to hear." It seems reasonable to conclude, however, that the stress difference was not heard by Sledd's informants because it was not there, and that Sledd and the others thought they heard it because they knew it was there in other contexts. This example thus seems to support Pike's and Bolinger's view of word stress as a "potential" entity and to cast further doubt on the existence of a clear-cut distinction between stress and pitch.

The simple sentences and phrases considered earlier in this chapter, then, indicate that a cyclic analysis of stress is at best beset with serious problems. The phenomenon discussed above would seem to suggest further that the cyclic approach accounts for something which does not exist: "preservation" of stress contours assigned smaller units when these occur in larger constructions. Both types of consideration thus point to the conclusion that English sentence-stress assignment is not cyclic, and that a new approach to sentence stress is in order.

2 Other Approaches to Sentence Stress

BRESNAN

It has long been noted that there are examples of "normal stress" which the NSR as formulated in *SPE* cannot account for. Perhaps the best-known such case is a contrast cited by Newman (1946), who observed that the stress contour of an expression like *instructions to leave* will vary according to different grammatical relations involved. Thus (52) is understood as (53), while (54) is understood as (55) (Newman's notation is used here):

(52) I have instrúctions to léave.
(53) I've been instructed to leave.

(54) I have instrúctions to lèave.
(55) I'm to leave instructions.

In a recent, widely reviewed paper, Bresnan (1971) attempts to account for this and other cases by ordering the NSR at the end of the syntactic cycle and by assuming that Question Formation and Relative Clause Formation are cyclic rules. Bresnan refers to her hypothesis concerning the ordering of the NSR as the *ordering hypothesis*, and the cases where her hypothesis permits the NSR to assign the correct stress contour involve movement or deletion of direct objects in embedded sentences and the difference between pronominal and full NPs. Thus, the contrast between (52) and (54) is accounted for, according to Bresnan, by the presence of an underlying direct object of *leave* in (54) but not in (52). If the NSR applies following all the syntactic rules on a given cycle, it will assign primary stress to this underlying occurrence of *instructions* on the lowest cycle, thereby reducing the stress on *leave*. Then, on the next cycle, this *instructions* will be deleted, and the NSR will place primary stress on the occurrence of *instructions* in the matrix sentence, since it will now bear the rightmost primary stress. Since (52) does not have a stressable direct object following *leave* in its underlying structure, on the other hand, the NSR will assign primary stress to *leave* on the lowest cycle, and *leave* will retain this primary stress throughout the derivation. A contrast like that between (56) and (57):

(56) George found someone he'd like you to m$\overset{1}{e}$et. (= Bresnan's [11a])
(57) George found some fr$\overset{1}{i}$ends he'd like you to meet. (= Bresnan's [11b])

is explained by Bresnan as being due to the nature of the relativized direct object: in (56) the embedded occurrence of *someone*, being pronominal, cannot be assigned primary stress, so the NSR will stress *meet*; this verb will not be deleted and will still bear the rightmost primary stress at the end of the next cycle. In (57), on the other hand, the NSR will assign primary stress to *friends* on the lowest cycle, thereby reducing the stress on *meet*. Thus, on the next cycle, after Relative Clause Formation has applied, the matrix *friends* will bear the rightmost primary stress and thus will again be assigned a primary stress by the NSR.

Although Bresnan does not make it clear in her prose, her analysis involves a fairly radical departure from the *SPE* analysis. While she assumes, like Chomsky and Halle, that the NSR can apply in any major constituent in isolation, she restricts its domain of application in the derivation of full sentences to NP and S, that is, those constituents which Chomsky (1970*b*) argues are the domain of the *syntactic* cycle. She thus accounts for the [231] contour in a sentence like (1) by assuming a [221] → [231] rule, which she does not, however, discuss in any detail. It becomes even clearer in her reply to her critics (Bresnan 1972) that she is not making any claims of generality for the NSR. Her important claim is, rather, that, regardless of what rules actually assign stress in simple sentences, the stress contours so assigned are "preserved through derivations."[1] Thus Bresnan's claim is independent of any claims concerning the viability of the NSR. There are, however, at least two ways in which her ordering hypothesis is vulnerable.

In the first place, the factual claim made by Bresnan's ordering hypothesis—that the stress contours of simple sentences are preserved through derivations—would appear to be falsified by the rhythm phe-

nomena discussed in Chapter 1. Recall that verb-particle cases like
(58) are not distinguished in terms of stress contour in simple sentences from verb + prepositional-phrase constructions like (59):

(58) I loŏked ŭp the ănswer.
(59) I wŏrked ŏn the ănswer.

Bresnan's ordering hypothesis thus predicts that if the final NP in
such examples is moved or deleted the resultant stress contour
should still be the same in the two types of construction. This is not
the case; the preposition in such a sentence will continue to exhibit
lower stress than the verb, but the particle will not:

(60) the ănswer I loŏked ŭp
(61) the ănswer I wŏrked ŏn

It would appear, then, that Bresnan can derive the correct stress contour in an example like (58) only by restricting whatever rule is responsible for the tertiary stress on particles in such examples to the
final domain of rule application—that is, to surface structure.[2] That
is, she would be forced to provide an ad hoc treatment of stress contours in verb-particle constructions which would falsify her ordering
hypothesis in its strongest form. As we shall see in Chapter 5, there is
an alternative analysis of stress which does not require an ad hoc
treatment of these constructions.

Even disregarding the problem presented by verb-particle constructions, however, Bresnan's ordering hypothesis is still vulnerable on
naturalness grounds. Note that Bresnan's analysis crucially involves a
stage in the derivation of sentences with relative clauses where relativized NPs are assigned primary stress. There are several considerations which lead to the conclusion that this is a highly questionable
stage.

Berman and Szamosi (1972:306, n. 2) point out that Bresnan's assumption that relative-clause formation consists in the deletion of a
full lexical noun phrase which is identical to the head is open to several objections. It is important to note that, even if these objections
can be countered in the case of Bresnan's examples, the objection to

the assignment of primary stress to relativized NPs remains. Bresnan's analysis claims that relativized NPs differ from anaphoric NPs in that the latter are not assigned primary stress, whereas the former are. As we shall see in Chapter 4, it is not true that anaphoric NPs are never stressed, but, since they are stressed only in certain situations which need not concern us here, I will in the present discussion engage in the convenient fiction that they are not stressed. (That is, I will refer to anaphoric NPs as generally not being stressed: this is to be taken as a shorthand expression for the situation discussed in Ch. 4.) While Bresnan is thus forced to treat anaphoric and relativized NPs in diametrically opposed ways, it is a fact that relativized NPs have much in common with anaphoric NPs. As is well known, for example, relativized NPs have properties of definite NPs even when their heads are indefinite. Several of these properties are discussed in Morgan 1972; to cite just one, the rule of *Tough*-Movement (Postal 1971) cannot move indefinite NPs:

> (62) It was impossible to lecture to the class.
> (63) The class was impossible to lecture to.
> (64) It was impossible to lecture to a class.
> (65) *A class was impossible to lecture to.

But *Tough*-Movement is not prevented from applying in the relative clause in (66) or (67), despite the fact that the head of this relative clause is indefinite:

> (66) A class that it was impossible to lecture to was the bane of my first year of teaching.
> (67) A class that was impossible to lecture to was the bane of my first year of teaching.

And just as relativized NPs are definite even when their heads are indefinite, an indefinite antecedent will be followed by a definite, not an indefinite, anaphor:

(68) I talked yesterday with an insurance salesman$_i$.

$$\left\{ \begin{array}{l} \text{He}_i \\ \text{The salesman}_i \\ \text{*One}_i \\ \text{*A salesman}_i \end{array} \right\} \text{tried to sell me a tax-sheltered annuity.}$$

Another way in which English relativized NPs are similar to anaphoric NPs is that they appear in a reduced form on the surface. Relative pronouns, like anaphoric pronouns, are unstressed. Bresnan does not mention relative clauses containing actual relative pronouns, but it is clear that in her analysis the treatment of sentences with them will not be as "neat." This is because examples containing relative pronouns pattern just like Bresnan's examples which contain no such elements:

(69) Here's something I just boúght.
(70) Here's something which I just boúght.

(71) Here's a boók I just bought.
(72) Here's a boók which I just bought.

Thus, to account for the second sentences in these pairs and the first sentences in a uniform fashion, Bresnan would have to permit derivations which included the following: (*a*) assignment of primary stress to NPs within relative clauses, (*b*) conversion of these NPs into relative pronouns, and (*c*) reduction of the stress on the relative pronouns. It thus appears to be an accident that relative pronouns are unstressed, just as anaphoric pronouns are. Such an analysis would claim, for example, that English might change through rule loss so that relative pronouns, but not anaphoric pronouns, were stressed.

It is instructive, in this context, to note examples of nonrestrictive relatives like (73):

(73) Bresnan's version of the NSR differs from that given in
    SPE, in which work the rule was first propósed.[1]

Examples like (73) are a paradigm case of stilted, literary style; sentences like this are learned quite late. Despite this, speakers know
how to pronounce them; no one would put primary stress on *work* in
this example. *Work* is treated here as we would expect an anaphoric
NP to be treated. While it is not clear from her discussion how Bresnan would treat nonrestrictive relative clauses, this example supports
the claim that it is a *general* property of English NPs which are not
"new" that they are not assigned primary stress. Thus, Bresnan's
analysis, in addition to making factual claims which are incorrect, involves a type of derivation which includes a highly artificial stage.

LAKOFF

Although Lakoff (1972) in his reply to Bresnan 1971 is concerned
primarily with the conclusions Bresnan draws from her analysis, he
also attempts a revision of the NSR which he intends to cover those
cases which Bresnan's treatment appears to handle successfully as
well as a number of additional cases which he claims are correctly
handled by the *SPE* treatment but not by Bresnan's. Lakoff argues
that sentences like (74) and (75) show that sentences with moved
postverbal NPs which are not direct objects (as the relevant NPs in
the examples Bresnan [1971] considered were) show stress contours
which would be assigned by a NSR which applied to surface structures:

(74) To what cíty was Jóhn tráveling? (= Lakoff's [40])
(75) From which aírport did Jóhn depárt? (= Lakoff's [41])

as do sentences like (76) and (77):

(76) Which pr$\overset{2}{\text{o}}$blems is it l$\overset{3}{\text{i}}$kely that he'll s$\overset{1}{\text{o}}$lve? (= Lakoff's [52])

(77) Which b$\overset{2}{\text{o}}$oks did Sam persuade H$\overset{3}{\text{a}}$rry to cr$\overset{1}{\text{i}}$ticize? (= Lakoff's [53])

Thus, while granting Bresnan the claim that the NSR must have access to structures obtaining before Relative Clause Formation and Question Formation have applied, Lakoff argues that sentences like (74)–(77) show that the rule must *apply* at the level of surface structure and, therefore, that the rule must be stated globally. Lakoff's final revision of the NSR is as follows (p. 298):

> In constituent A, put *1*-stress on constituent B if
> (a) B is stressable; and either
> (b) in logical structure B is a direct object, and in shallow structure B has no clausemates following it, and in surface structure B is a clausemate of its logical predicate P; or
> (c) there is no constituent to the right of B bearing *1*-stress.

(where the "direct object of a 2-place or 3-place atomic predicate is defined as that atomic predicate's last argument" [p. 295, n. 6], and where the word *or* is taken as imposing disjunctive ordering). Thus, (b) is intended to cover those cases where Bresnan's analysis predicts what Lakoff considers to be the correct stress contour, whereas (c) corresponds to the *SPE* statement of the NSR.

Since Lakoff's revision of the NSR is predicated on the assumption that the cyclic approach of *SPE* is essentially valid, the objections presented against that approach in Chapter 1 pertain equally well to his revision. An additional problem for Lakoff's revision is provided by a set of sentences pointed out by Berman and Szamosi (1972) which pattern like those discussed in Bresnan 1971 but where it is the *subject* of the embedded S which is moved or deleted; such cases are illustrated by (78)–(83):

(78) Let me tell you about something that h$\overset{1}{\text{a}}$ppened. (= Berman and Szamosi's [1])

(79) Let me tell you about something str$\overset{1}{\text{a}}$nge that happened. (= Berman and Szamosi's [2])

(80) Mary liked the propósal that was made. (= Berman and
Szamosi's [5])

(81) John asked what bóoks had been written. (= Berman and
Szamosi's [6a])
(82) John asked what bóoks had arrived. (= Berman and Szamosi's [6b])

(83) There is wórk to be done. (= Berman and Szamosi's [10])

Lakoff thus appears to have been mistaken in his assumption that the
direct-object relation was crucial in the sentences which Bresnan
1971 appeared to handle correctly.[3]

Disregarding the counterexamples, there are problems with Lakoff's rule itself. The most serious problems involve the question of
interpreting the global conditions. Since, in the sort of logical structure Lakoff appears to envisage in his other works, the NPs which are
to be assigned stress by (b) "correspond" to predicates which, in the
course of a derivation, are substituted for indices, it is not clear how
to interpret the condition that "constituent B" must be a "direct object" in logical structure: B would appear to be a predicate itself in
logical structure. A similar problem shows up in the condition that B
must be a clausemate of "its logical predicate P" in surface structure.
It is not clear how this condition is to be interpreted in a theory like
Lakoff's which permits lexical decomposition, since, in such a theory, "constituent B" may in surface structure be the moved direct object of a verb which has been substituted for a structure arising through
the application of Predicate Raising. In such a sentence B's "logical
predicate P" does not directly correspond to a predicate in surface
structure. Perhaps fortunately, this is a moot point: this last condition, which Lakoff added to prevent (b) from applying in sentences
like (76) and (77), will also prevent (b) from applying in relative-
clause cases like (84):

(84) I gave John the bóoks he wanted. (= Lakoff's [58])

since *the books* is not a clausemate of *wanted* in surface structure.

Even if the mechanical problems in Lakoff's revised NSR could be corrected, however, the rule remains at best a list of observations.[4] Given this and all the problems it inherits from the *SPE* analysis, it seems pointless to try to revise the rule further.[5]

BOLINGER

The approaches of Bresnan and Lakoff to sentence stress have in common an underlying assumption that there is a systematic relationship between the structure of an utterance and its stress—an assumption which, as we have seen, has been widely held in American linguistics. One American linguist who has refused to accept this assumption is Dwight Bolinger, who has argued (1958*a*; 1972) that it is the speaker's intent, rather than the structure of the sentence, that determines stress placement (or what he refers to as "sentence accents"). Bolinger's position is illustrated well by the following passage:

> My position was—and is—that the location of sentence accents is not explainable by syntax or morphology. . . . I have held, with Hultzén 1956, that what item "has relatively stronger stress [accent] in the larger intonational pattern is a matter of information, not of structure" (199). . . .
> Following are examples in which the Nuclear Stress Rule (NSR) as modified [by Bresnan (1971)] ought to eliminate the accent on the final verb, but either does not or need not. They are matched with others where the rule operates successfully. The point of the comparison is the nature of the verbs as lexical items:
>
> > The end of the chapter is reserved for various pròblems to compúterize.
> > The end of the chapter is reserved for various próblems to solve.
> > I have a pòint to émphasize.

I have a póint to make.

I can't finish in an hour —there are simply too many tòpics to elúcidate.

I can't finish in an hour –there are simply too many tópics to cover.

Knowing his character you can guess what he's up to— probably looking for some poor bòob to chéat.

I'm hot. I'm looking for sòmething còol to drínk.

Next month we may bc out on the street. I'm looking for a hóuse to rent.

By contrasting items like *computerize* and *solve*, *elucidate* and *cover*, I do not mean to suggest that one can predict with assurance that one will be accented and the other not. I only emphasize that this is one factor in the speaker's decision. When he decides to say *elucidate* rather than *cover*, he has already made up his mind that the operation rather than the thing is the point of information focus; the choice of the semantically richer verb is part of the decision. He could decide, though this is less likely, to accent the semantically poorer word (*discuss* would be a better candidate for this than *cover*), or to de-accent the richer one. The latter would be true of *bòob to chéat* (reducing it to *bóob to cheat*) but less likely of *sòmething còol to drínk*, and this reflects the meaning of the sentence as a whole, especially as influenced by the main verb. *Look for* opens up possibilities that are somewhat obstructed by presentative verbs like *I have* and *there is*, which tend to focus on the noun, exactly as presentative *came* focuses on the noun in *Then the wínds came*.

Some unattested historical episodes by way of further illustration.

Boston Strangler, out for his first prowl: Where can I find a gìrl to strángle?

Matthew: What is Jesus doing this afternoon? Mark: He is looking for a còuple of dèad men to resurréct.

Sigmund Freud: On your way back, bring me a pàtient to psychoánalyse.

Daniel Ellsberg: I've got these pàpers to declássify.
Sir Galahad: I'll be late for tea. I have a couple of làdies in
distrèss to réscue.
Thomas Arnold, Rugby, 1828: Tell Mary I'll be along in a
minute. First I have a bòy to cáne.

If Arnold had been seeing the boy rather than caning him, he
probably would have said *bóy to see*.[1] [Bolinger's n. 1 discusses
some examples in Lakoff 1972 which need not concern us
here.]

The error of attributing to syntax what belongs to semantics
comes from concentrating on the commonplace. In phrases like
bóoks to write, *wórk to do*, *clóthes to wear*, *fóod to eat*, *léssons
to learn*, *gróceries to get*—as they occur in most contexts—the
verb is highly predictable: food is to eat, clothes are to wear,
work is to do, lessons are to learn. Less predictable verbs are less
likely to be de-accented—where one has *léssons to learn*, one
will probably have *pàssages to mémorize*. It is only incidental
that the syntax favors one or the other accent pattern. *It's time
to léave* speaks of leaving; a paraphrase is *We must leave*. *I have
a dúty to perform* speaks of duty; the verb could be omitted
and the meaning would be the same. (Bolinger 1972:633–634)

Bolinger's work, then, contains two important claims concerning
sentence stress. One is a negative claim: that there is no systematic
relationship between the structure of an utterance and its stress contour.[6] Bolinger summarizes this claim as follows:

The distribution of sentence accents is not determined by syntactic structure but by semantic and emotional highlighting.
Syntax is relevant indirectly in that some structures are more
likely to be highlighted than others. But a description along
these lines can only be in statistical terms. Accents should not
be mashed down to the level of [word] stresses, which are lexical abstractions. In their zeal to reverse Trager-Smith phonology, transformationalists have fallen into the same trap. Whether
one tries to set up prosodic rules for syntax or syntactic rules

for prosody, the result is the same: two domains are confused which should be kept apart. (1972:644)

Bolinger's positive claim is summarized in the abstract to Bolinger 1972 thus: "Accented words are points of information focus." As the passage from Bolinger 1972 quoted at the beginning of this section indicates, Bolinger is arguing that the relatively more unpredictable items in an utterance are more likely to be stressed, a claim which is illustrated further in the following:

It is not necessary for the verb to be fully predictable from the noun; what counts is RELATIVE semantic weight. For this it is necessary to take account of the entire context, including the context of situation. . . . It is easy to create a situation in which *What kíngs abdicated* is normal and noncontrastive: *I don't care how many passengers were rescued from the Titanic. At that point in history what I want to know is what kíngs abdicated.* The speaker is interested in the fate of kings and the rise of democracies. There is enough mutual understanding between him and his interlocutor to make him reasonably sure that the mention of "kings"—in the context of democracy—will suggest "abdication." (Bolinger 1972:635)

Bolinger's examples illustrate the first of these claims very well—and, as we shall see in Chapter 4, there is abundant additional evidence which can be adduced to show that a theory which attempts to deal with stress assignment in purely structural terms is forced to make either false or vacuous claims. Since, to the best of my knowledge, Bolinger's second claim is the only alternative seriously proposed to a structural treatment in American linguistics, it is worth investigating whether it provides us with a more promising approach. Unfortunately, Bolinger's claim (as I understand it) appears to make the wrong predictions in a number of cases.

Recall Bolinger's account of the stress in his example *what kíngs abdicated*: his claim is that this clause with this stress contour will be uttered in a context where the speaker can assume that the mention of kings will suggest "abdication." Yet it is easy to construct a number of simple subject–intransitive-verb sentences where the primary stress falls on the subject, yet where the verb does not seem to be at all "predictable":

(33) Hey—your cóat's on fire!
(85) I'm not going to be able to make it in today—the cár blew up.
(86) My wátch stopped. Do you know what time it is?
(87) Your wífe called. Your uncle Hárry died, and the táx people want to see you.

On the other hand, the predicates in the following examples do seem to be reasonably "predictable"; yet they are stressed:

(88) Come on in—the dôor's ópen.
(89) I was afraid to get any more explicit because the phône is tápped.
(90) Well, just make sure you don't get caught. Driving without a license is illégal.

A particularly telling pair of examples showing the inadequacy of a theory which attempts to account for stress in this way can be found in the recent reports of the deaths of two former presidents as I heard them; the examples are worth discussing in some detail. In December of 1972 former president Truman was hospitalized in critical condition. He remained in the hospital for some time, and daily reports concerning his now critical, now serious, now critical condition were given in the news media. Because of the seriousness of Truman's condition and his advanced age, it could reasonably be assumed that he would not survive this crisis and that it was just a matter of time before he would die. At the time when Truman finally did die, I was visiting my parents; one morning I came downstairs to breakfast, and my mother, who had gotten up earlier and listened to the news, announced to me:

(91) Trûman díed.

A few weeks later I was back at my job at the University of Texas. One afternoon my husband drove to campus to pick me up when I was finished working for the day, and as I got into the car he announced:

    (92) Jóhnson dîed.

Though Johnson's health had been in the news some time previously, he was apparently recovering from the heart attack he had had, and his condition had ceased to be newsworthy. (In fact, the most recent news concerning Johnson had been his attendance at a civil rights conference at the LBJ Library in Austin.) Johnson's health was not on people's minds as Truman's had been, and when his death came it was a surprise.

What is significant for the present discussion is the difference in the contexts in which these two reports were uttered: Truman's death was expected; Johnson's was not. Bolinger's theory would appear to suggest, however, that the mention of Truman in the relevant context should have suggested "death" and, therefore, that *died* in (91) should not be stressed. On the other hand, the mention of Johnson in the relevant context should not have suggested "death" any more than anything else one might have wanted to say about him, and therefore *died* in (92) *should* be stressed. Bolinger's theory would thus appear to predict stress contours opposite to the ones which actually occurred.

It is interesting to note that the bulk of examples that Bolinger actually discusses are of one syntactic type—"infinitival relatives"—and it is in his discussion of these examples that his account seems most persuasive. Yet, as he states his principle involving relative semantic weight, it would appear to be inaccurate for this type of case as well. C. L. Baker has pointed out to me a context in which such an example might be uttered where the noun would be stressed, even though it would appear to be more "predictable" than the verb (personal communication, 1973). The context is this: Suppose I operate a small shrimp-processing plant. Shrimp are the only things which are processed at this plant, but, of course, the processing involves doing several different things to the shrimp. Now suppose that some afternoon I am busy working and a friend drops by and invites me to go out for a beer. I reply:

(93) I can't—I've got all these shrímp to $\begin{Bmatrix} \text{clean} \\ \text{sort} \\ \text{peel} \\ \text{devein} \\ \text{package} \\ \text{etc.} \end{Bmatrix}$

Clearly, in this context, there are a variety of verbs which might appear in an utterance like (93), whereas *shrimp* is almost completely "predictable": it would appear to be the case that the verb in such an example is conveying more information than *shrimp*. Yet (93) indicates the natural pronunciation for this type of sentence in this context: primary stress on the verb would sound quite odd.

The types of examples discussed above would seem to suggest very strongly, then, that "relative semantic weight" is not the crucial factor in the assignment of stress in such utterances. An additional problem appears in certain cases which have a primary stress on an item which appears to be conveying little if any information at all; an example of this sort of case is (94):

(94) John is a wônderful mán.

Clearly, sentence (94) involves an assertion concerning John's character; *man* seems to add hardly any information. Some more examples of this type follow:

(95) That was a delîcious dínner.
(96) *The Godfather* is really a gôry móvie.
(97) Champaign-Urbana is a delîghtful pláce.

The same sort of observation can be made concerning a sentence which Bolinger (1972:635) himself cites as an example showing that more than one "main accent" may occur in a sentence (Bolinger's notation is used here):

(98) George is a wónderful fríend to háve.

Here, again, *to have* seems to be adding virtually no information to the utterance; why should it receive a primary stress?[7]

Of the two significant claims which Bolinger makes, then, one—that sentence stress assignment is not a function of syntactic structure—seems to be solid. The second claim—that those items which have relatively more "weight" are stressed—appears to encounter serious problems. An alternative approach to sentences such as those discussed here is presented in Chapter 5.

3 The Normal-Stress Notion

Generative grammarians have assumed that normal stress and nonnormal stress are to be assigned by quite different processes—and, in the few studies of sentence stress done in this framework, only normal stress has been dealt with, perhaps on the assumption that nonnormal stress is to be described as a deviation from the norm, thus presupposing an adequate account of normal stress. While this assumption of a strict dichotomy of processes has rarely been made explicit,[1] it seems to be generally held.[2] Thus several of the replies to Bresnan (1971) adduce "wrong predictions" made by her analysis. These "wrong predictions" are in most cases perfectly acceptable sentences; what is "wrong" with them is that they involve stress felt to be contrastive, and thus it is assumed that her analysis should *not* predict them. The following are typical of this kind of criticism:

> One can dream up indefinitely many examples . . . in which the noncontrastive contour center location is on the last accentable item of the relative clause. All of them should be instances of CONTRASTIVE stress, under Bresnan's hypothesis . . . (Stockwell 1971:34–35)

> In the following examples, 38 is the typical case that [Bresnan's] analysis covers. The rest are cases where her analysis yields the wrong result. I will use the asterisk to indicate that the sentence with the stress given is incorrect in my idiolect on a NON-CONTRASTIVE, NON-EMPHATIC reading, though it may be all right on contrastive or emphatic readings, or in other idiolects. (Lakoff 1972:294)

> The stress patterns of all these sentences are cases of normal, non-contrastive, non-emphatic stress. Most people find that shifting the primary stress to final position in the cases given

Note: An earlier version of this chapter appeared in *Language*, 1974, *50*, 66–73, under the title "A Re-examination of 'Normal Stress'."

> earlier, or conversely, shifting it to the head noun (or ques-
> tioned noun) in 22–24, results in sentences that are distinctly
> odd. (Of course, they can all be given contrastive interpreta-
> tions, in which case there is nothing strange about them.) (Ber-
> man and Szamosi 1972:312–313)[3]

Note that any investigation of the adequacy of any rules meant to
account for normal stress presupposes an independent definition of
normal stress; without this, the claims embodied by such rules have
no empirical basis.

Reference to normal stress appears frequently in works on syntax
where stress itself is not the object of investigation. Syntacticians are
all familiar with statements like the following:

> . . . even richly inflected languages do not seem to tolerate reor-
> dering when it leads to ambiguity. Thus in a German sentence
> such as *"Die Mutter sieht die Tochter,"* in which the inflections
> do not suffice to indicate grammatical function, it seems that
> the interpretation will invariably be that *"Die Mutter"* is the
> Subject (unless it has contrastive stress, in which case it may be
> taken to be the Subject or the Object). The same seems to be
> true in other languages as diverse as Russian . . . and Mohawk.
> In the latter, the Verb contains affixes designating the Subject
> and Object, but where the reference is ambiguous, the initial NP
> is taken to be the Subject, under normal intonation. (Chomsky
> 1965:126–127)[4]

Some more examples follow:

> Perhaps the most fundamental untreated problem concerning
> the cross-over principle is that provided by examples with con-
> trastive stress. It was observed at the very beginning of this
> study . . . for example, that reflexive passives, which are ill
> formed when the reflexive word has ordinary stress, are well
> formed when contrastive stress occurs on this element. (Postal
> 1971:230)

A question like:

19. (28) Who did Charley insult?

with ordinary stress throughout *cannot* be answered with a sentence like:

19. (19) Charley insulted his father.

with ordinary stress throughout. Rather, it must be answered by a sentence like:

19. (20) Charley insulted his *father*.

with contrastive stress on that NP which "corresponds" to the "questioned" NP in the question sentence. (Postal 1971: 234)

. . . these regularities are influenced in a complex way by stress and intonation. As I cannot go into these phenomena here, I will only consider examples which are neutral in this respect, that is, which show neither marked stress differences between the elements in question nor any special type of intonation. Under such conditions, the abovementioned connection between surface order and meaning comes out quite clearly. (Schiebe 1970: 351, n. 1)

. . . while (1a) can be converted into (1b),

(1) a. I expect him to be there at midnight.
    b. At midnight I expect him to be there.

(2a) cannot be converted into (2b), unless the preposed adverb is contrastively stressed.

(2) a. I expected him to [be there at midnight].
    b. *At midnight I expected him to be there. (Postal and Ross 1970: 145)

Notice, once again, that all such statements presuppose an independent definition of "normal stress," "contrastive stress," and so on.
  The difficulties involved with the notion of normal stress are nice-

ly underscored by a statement made by Chomsky, Halle, and Lukoff. Having stated that they "have excluded from consideration all forms of expressive stress, including contrastive stress," where "expressive elements" are defined as "deviations from the normal pattern," they state:

> It should be noted that as a consequence of our decision to exclude contrastive stress from consideration we do not provide for the normal stress patterns of such utterances as "This is the brown house, not the white one," where there is extra heavy stress and extra high pitch on "brown" and "white." The description of such utterances poses many problems which have never been adequately handled. We feel that these utterances are best regarded as being in a special sense deviations from the normal pattern, and that a satisfactory description of them will require the development of methods not currently in use in phonemics. (1956:78)

This comes dangerously close to circularity: one seems to be saying, "My rules account for normal stress, and 'normal stress' means the stress my rules predict." It might be argued, of course, that this is a perfectly possible definition of normal stress; that the term is just a convenient abbreviation, with no circularity involved at all. It seems, in fact, that Chomsky is using the term in just this way when he refers to "normal intonation" as "the intonation defined by the regular processes described in Chomsky and Halle (1968)." (Chomsky 1970a, reprinted in Steinberg and Jakobovits, eds. 1971:203).[5] However, aside from the problem this poses for empirical confirmation of the validity of the rules in question, it is evident that Chomsky, like other linguists, is assuming an independent characterization of the different types of intonation referred to; elsewhere in the paper he refers to special semantic properties of sentences with "contrastive stress." Note that the passage from Chomsky 1965 cited above, which refers to contrastive stress in German and normal intonation in Mohawk, would appear to presuppose a language-independent characterization of these concepts. It is clear that this "convenient-abbreviation" definition of normal stress is of no linguistic interest.

It has apparently been generally assumed that every sentence has a "normal" pronunciation and that any special prosodic properties can be described in terms of deviations from this norm. Such was apparently the position of Trager and Smith, who introduced the shift-morpheme:

> In a phrase like *I don't know* we may have various superfixes: /ày+donów/, /ày+dòwnt+nów/, /ày+dównt+nôw/, /áy+dòwnt+nôw/. The statistically most frequent and most "neutral" way of saying it is the first; the second is also frequent, especially in "careful" speech. But the last two are examples of a phenomenon that can be analyzed only as secondary to the first two examples. They exhibit a SHIFT of stress from the "normal" final position back toward the beginning of the phrase. It may be concluded that there are shift-morphemes, or a shift-morpheme with allomorphs, differing by the position that the primary stress takes in relation to its "normal" position . . . (1951:72–73)

Recently, this assumption has been stated explicitly by Stockwell, who asserts that "there is such a thing as a 'neutral' or 'normal' or 'colorless' intonation for any sentence, serving as a baseline against which all other possible contours are contrastable, and thereby meaningful" (1971:25). While I applaud Stockwell's unfortunately almost unique recognition of the necessity for making such assumptions explicit, it is easy to show that this assumption is mistaken. Two examples should suffice:

(99) Even a two-year-old could do that.
(100) John was killed by himself.

These sentences *must* have what would generally be referred to today as contrastive stress on *two-year-old* and *himself*, respectively. (I hasten to point out that such sentences are fairly well known.) If they are to be described as exhibiting a "shift in the intonation center," the question immediately arises: shift from what?

If we ask why a "normal" stress contour is impossible for these sentences, the answer that comes to mind is this: it is impossible to utter such sentences without making special assumptions. Is "normal" stress, then, the stress a speaker uses when making no special assumptions? Here we get back to the problem raised in Chapter 1 by sentences like (29), *John died*. Which of the pronunciations given in (101) and (102) is normal?

(101) Jôhn díed.
(102) Jóhn dîed.

In Chapter 1 we temporarily "solved" this problem by asserting that (102) was normal, since (101) involved the special assumption that John's death was in a sense foreseeable. There is, however, another context in which (101) is used: as an answer by an informant to the question *How would you pronounce (29)?* (When I mentioned the matter of context and special assumptions to my informants, the response would be an amazed *Hey—you're right!*) The answer to the question of what "normal" stress is, then, seems to be "stress used in citations." This, in fact, is exactly what Stockwell maintained at the Second Texas Conference. He stated:

> When utterances are elicited from an informant, certain intonation patterns regularly occur. These are citation patterns. They can be re-elicited from any number of informants with almost perfect consistency. They are also heard in normal discourse, but no sampling or statistical work of any sort has been done to indicate whether such patterns are the most frequent ones or not. It is true, however, that where they are observed in normal discourse, they can be shown by questioning to carry no additional component or differential meaning beyond that which is assignable to the segmental morphemes alone. Such patterns may, for convenience, be labelled "normal." (Hill 1962*b*:100)

This is probably the position that has been tacitly assumed by generative grammarians. While accepting citation stress as "normal," linguists have apparently simply assumed that this was also the least marked stress of discourse and failed to notice the *John died* dilemma.

What must be asked now is whether this exalted status should be accorded citations. It might be claimed that it should be, that citations show a certain pristine stress contour since they are, in fact, contextless. There are two objections to this approach, which really collapse into one. The first objection—the quibble—is that not all citations are really contextless. *John died* is about as contextless as a sentence can get. Substitute *my physics professor* for *John*, and the informant responses change. Apparently it is easier to imagine having a physics professor than it is to imagine knowing this *John* of linguistic example-sentence fame. An analogous but more striking example has been pointed out to me by James McCawley (personal communication, 1972): (103) gives the title of a character in Joseph Heller's *Catch-22*, generally cited as indicated in (104), with what might be described as an enumeration contour:

(103) Major Major Major Major
(104) Mâjor Mâjor Mâjor Májor

Of course, the "real-life" pronunciation would be something like that indicated in (105), parallel to that in (106):

(105) Màjor Mâjor Màjor Májor.
(106) Gèneral Dwîght Dàvid Éisenhower

I doubt very much that any informant would claim to pronounce the latter as in (107):

(107) Gêneral Dwîght Dâvid Éisenhower

—although a beginning reader might well *read* it that way out loud, being still at a stage of trying to recognize representations of individual words.

What examples like these show is this: a linguist who wishes to consider language in a vacuum and base an analysis of English stress on citations will have to claim that the difference between the stress contours in (104) and (106) represents a fact about English. It should be clear, however, that the difference in stress contours is due to facts about the world and not to a property of the grammar of English.

The real objection, then, is this: the more a citation is divorced from context, the more it is divorced from semantics—the utterer of the citation is not producing a real, natural-language sentence with both a phonetic and a semantic representation; he is producing a string of phones. Putting an example sentence in a context forces an informant to consider what the sentence means. I do not mean to suggest here that contexts are included in the semantic representation of sentences; I am simply suggesting that it is possible for an informant to deal with an example sentence without any consideration of its meaning, just as it is possible to read a sentence off a printed page without understanding it. When a context—or part of a context—is introduced, the informant must start to consider the meaning of the sentence.

If normal stress, then, means the stress assigned a contextless citation, it means the stress assigned a sentence with no semantic representation. This is not altogether surprising, in view of the fact that the notion of normal stress was inherited from a school which held that semantics was excluded from the realm of grammar. In fact, the notion of normal stress was probably necessitated by this very assumption, since any stress contours deemed to be of grammatical significance had to be distinguished from those of purely semantic significance. In Trager and Smith's framework, "normal" stress contours had to be determined before syntax could be done, since these were used in their immediate constituent analysis. Needless to say, the assumptions of the generative framework are quite inconsistent with those of Trager and Smith. Yet, even though their notion of "normal stress" is inconsistent with generative grammarians' assumptions, the latter have continued to accept it—and, unlike linguists working in the earlier framework, ceased to question what it means.

It may well be, of course, that some linguists will want to continue to accept the citation-stress definition of normal stress, claiming that such stress is in some sense basic and ignoring the problem that many sentences would have no "normal" stress contour and the problem that there is apparently no direct relationship between amount of deviation from the "norm" and the number of special assumptions made by the speaker of a sentence. Such an assumption, taken seriously, would of course divorce normal stress not only from semantics but from much of syntax as well. Furthermore, despite Stockwell's statement cited above, it is unlikely that informant responses would really be consistent, since some informants seem to put example sentences in context, as it were, more than others.[6] As noted, it is very difficult *not* to put some expressions in a context. Berman and Szamosi also noted this fact; they state: ". . . speakers asked to read aloud the sentence *Whose country did Nepal invade?* invariably put primary stress on *Nepal*. It would seem, then, that the normal stress contour of the above sentence is that in which the subject is stressed. It is clear that this is so only with reference to facts about the world" (1972:314, n. 11). Since citations have in a real sense a marginal status as natural-language *sentences* (as opposed to strings of phones) I would argue that the stress used in them should also be considered to have a marginal linguistic status.

Before continuing, I want to mention two possible objections that might be made to this conclusion and explain why I think they are not real objections. The first objection might be that the differences between citation stress and real-context stress are part of the difference between competence and performance and that I am denying that such a distinction exists. I do not wish to deny a distinction between speakers' knowledge of their language and their use of that and other knowledge in actual production and perception of utterances: what I want to emphasize here is that knowledge of the difference between citation stress and real-context stress is part of the linguistic competence of any native speaker. Notice that speakers are able to tell, for example, whether an interview on television is spontaneous or whether the participants have memorized their lines or are reading them from cue cards. Notice further that speakers may say of a bad actor, "He sounds as if he were reading his lines." Observations such as these show that speakers do have a knowledge of this difference; on what basis are they able to make such judgments if not their linguistic competence?

The second objection that might be made is that I am declaring citation stress to be uninteresting by fiat; that it too is part of our linguistic behavior and should be accounted for. This I would not deny —and, in fact, I believe that the facts concerning citation stress itself support the claims made above. Trager and Smith's claim that the primary stress will come "as near the end as possible," when viewed as an observation about citation stress, seems to be part of a more general phenomenon. To see this, consider phrases like the following:

(108) for Pete's sake
(109) yes, sir
(110) the lion's share

Each of these phrases is ambiguous as written between what we shall refer to as an idiomatic reading and a literal reading. What is interesting about these phrases for the present discussion is that the stress contours they display differ according to which reading is involved. As Green (1973) observes, an expression like (108) will have primary stress on *Pete's* on the literal reading but on *sake* on the idiomatic reading; thus compare (111) with (112):

(111) For Péte's sake, George ought to stop seeing Pete's wife.
(112) For Pete's sáke, shut the goddam door!!

Similarly, when an expression like (109) is used as a polite reply the primary stress will fall on *yes*; *sir*, like any vocative in a context like this, will not be stressed. When this phrase is an expression of enthusiasm, however, the pronunciation is as in (113):[7]

(113) yêssír

Finally, the phrase in (110) is pronounced by many speakers as in (114) when it means "the share belonging to the lion" but as in (115) when it means, roughly, "the largest portion":

(114) the líon's share
(115) the lion's sháre

What these examples have in common is that in their literal, analyzable meaning primary stress does not come at the end; in their unanalyzable use primary stress *does* come at the end. These phrases would seem, then, to illustrate a general principle; in an unanalyzable expression the greatest stress goes at the end. "Pure" citations—strings of phones not related to a semantic representation—have this same property of unanalyzability; thus the stress used in them seems to be part of a larger phenomenon. This then is further evidence that citations should be kept distinct from actual sentences, in the sense used above.

The following question now arises: is some other definition of normal stress possible which would provide us with a useful concept? The definition "stress used in a neutral context" comes to mind. But notice that there is no such thing as a totally neutral context. What may seem like the normal stress contour for a given sentence in a "neutral" context may change when some new lexical item is substituted for one in the original sentence, simply because of facts of the world with respect to the referents of these lexical items. Thus, consider (116) and (117), which might be considered to have the normal stress for a neutral context:

(116) This is the măn I was télling you about.
(117) This is the dóctor I was telling you about.

Notice that the question of special speaker assumptions does not enter into this stress difference in any immediately obvious way: I can stress (116) as indicated even if my addressee did not know in advance that the person in question was a man, and I can stress (117) as indicated even if the addressee knew that the person in question was a doctor. But now suppose I am in an environment where men are quite rare. I would stress the first sentence as in (118):

(118) This is the mán I was telling you about.

Likewise, if I work in a hospital, and am talking to another hospital employee, in the hospital, I am likely to stress the second sentence as in (119):

(119) This is the dŏctor I was télling you about.

Clearly, special assumptions *do* play a role here: assumptions involving the "remarkableness" of the referents of the NPs in question. Note that *lexical* properties of the NPs are not the crucial factor here.

The suggestion that there is no such thing as an absolutely neutral context should not be surprising in view of the fact that sentences have meaning. In a generative framework, where it is held that a grammar relates sound and meaning, there is no a priori reason to suppose that meaning should be relevant to stress assignment in some sentences but not in others.

In fact, even our old friend *John died* shows how careful we must be when talking about neutral contexts and special assumptions: even this simple sentence presupposes that there is—or was—some individual named John, known to the speaker and addressee(s). Thus the neutral-context definition of "normal stress," too, is unworkable.

It remains true that some utterance-tokens involve more special assumptions than others, and linguists can profitably study the effects different assumptions have on stress, just as we can study what effects various syntactic and phonological properties of utterances may have on stress. But it is not obvious that adopting a notion like "normal stress" is going to prove useful; it is more likely that it can only blind us to properties of the sentences we label "normal."[8]

4 The Question of Stressability

It was suggested in Chapter 3 that there appears to be a correlation between whether or not a noun phrase is heavily stressed in a given utterance, on the one hand, and whether or not the speaker assumes the referent of that noun phrase to be "remarkable" in the context in which the utterance is made, on the other. It is probably safe to assume that no linguist has ever wished to deny any such statement in the course of making factual claims concerning sentence stress; on the other hand, the formal statements linguists have made within some theoretical framework concerning the "stressability" of particular items in an utterance have been of a fundamentally different nature from such informal observations. It has been claimed rather that there is a direct correlation between the stressability of items and their category membership. Thus, for example, it has been claimed that, in cases of "normal" stress, nouns are among the categories which are assigned stress, whereas pronouns are not. While it has been recognized that there are indeed utterances in which pronouns appear stressed and utterances in which nouns appear unstressed, it has been claimed that some special phenomenon is involved in these latter cases which is not involved in the "normal" cases. One such special phenomenon which is frequently referred to in a casual manner is "contrastive stress."

In this chapter claims concerning correlations between the stressing of items and their category membership are critically examined, with special reference to stressing of nouns and pronouns. The first section is a review of the facts concerning these phenomena, and it is argued that any theory which claims such correlations between stressability and category membership is forced to make either false or empirically vacuous claims. This position rests on the claim that no independent characterization of any "special" phenomena concerning stress assignment can be given. The second section is devoted

Note: An earlier version of part of this chapter appeared in "Contrastive Stress and Semantic Relations," in *Papers from the Tenth Regional Meeting, Chicago Linguistic Society*, ed. M. W. LaGaly, R. A. Fox, and A. Bruck (Chicago: Chicago Linguistic Society, 1974), pp. 608–616.

to an examination of the viability of one such phenomenon, "contrastive stress." It is shown that "contrastive stress" is a notion which different writers have used in different ways and which eludes any precise characterization. The third section of this chapter attempts an informal characterization of "stressability" of various items in an utterance, and the theoretical implications of the informal conclusions of the third section are examined in the fourth section.

STRESSING OF NOUNS AND PRONOUNS

It will be recalled that Trager and Smith's claim that the primary stress of a "phonemic phrase" will come at the end was qualified with the phrase "as near as possible." Specifically, "some items, such as pronoun objects, certain adverbs, prepositions, and others, do not have primary stress though they are normally the last thing in a phrase, and they get primary stress only with the shift-morpheme" (Trager and Smith 1951:75). This statement would seem to be equivalent to the statement that pronouns (and members of certain other categories) receive primary stress only in cases which are not "normal." Translating into generative terms, we can say that this statement is equivalent to the claim that pronouns (and members of other relevant categories) are not assigned stress by the same rules that assign stress in "normal" cases. This seems to be the generally held assumption.[1]

It is important to emphasize exactly what is being claimed by authors who make this assumption. The most obvious interpretation of what are by now traditional claims concerning the stressability of nouns and pronouns is that nouns are always stressed and that pronouns are never stressed, and it is obvious that, under such an interpretation, such claims are patently false. Sentences (120) and (121) are clear examples of cases where nouns are not stressed, and (122) and (123) are clear cases of stressed pronouns:

(120) This is the măn (wŏman, chăracter, etc.) I was télling you about.

(121) I'd give the money to Máry, but I don't trúst Măry.

(122) Put it next to hím.

(123) There must be sómeone who can figure out what to do.

Examples such as these are well known, and the authors of statements concerning a direct correlation between stressability of items and their category membership were well aware of them. They thus modified their claims in the following way: the "normal" or unmarked state of affairs is for nouns to be stressed and for pronouns not to be stressed. If we encounter an unstressed noun or a stressed pronoun, then we can be sure that we are dealing with some special phenomenon. For Trager and Smith the special phenomenon was the shift-morpheme; for Chomsky and Halle it was some sort of coding mechanism which would mark certain items in surface structure as not being subject to the rules for "normal" stress assignment.[2]

Trager and Smith and Chomsky and Halle do not discuss the question of whether the special phenomena they assume to operate in cases of unstressed nouns or stressed pronouns have any independent characterization, but it is clear that, if their claims are intended to have any empirical validity, some such independent characterization must exist. Otherwise such claims reduce to statements like "The primary stress of a phonemic phrase comes at the end except when it doesn't," "Nouns are always stressed except when they aren't," and so on.[3] One must therefore assume that such authors have indeed assumed some such independent characterizations. Thus, it might be claimed, the nouns in example (120) fail to be stressed because of some lexical peculiarity they possess which correlates with their low semantic content. This is the approach taken by Bresnan, who refers to "semi-pronouns like *people, things*" in a discussion of items which she claims are not stressed by the NSR (1971:271), and, as indicated in Chapter 3, such a claim is untenable, since whether or not a noun is stressed in such a sentence correlates with the context in which it is uttered. Another claim with a similar status which is implied in many works is that *Mary* in (121) is unstressed because it is anaphoric, whereas *him* in (122) is stressed because it is *not* anaphoric but deictic. It is indeed interesting to note that such informal statements have been made by many who maintain the position that there is a direct correlation between stressability and category membership, even though such informal statements imply something quite different: that the significant correlation is between stressability and anaphoricity, not between stressability and category membership. Though this is indeed a remarkable state of affairs,[4] the implication of such informal statements, taken alone, is false: anaphoric items, whether nouns or pronouns, can indeed be stressed, as in examples (124) and (125):

> (124) I know who's standing in front of Máry, but I don't know who Máry's in front of.
> (125) I know who's standing in front of Máry, but I don't know who shé's in front of.

Examples such as these are frequently referred to as exhibiting another special phenomenon, contrastive stress.

So far, the examples we have considered suggest that the claims made concerning stressability of nouns and pronouns are on shaky ground. Members of both categories may appear stressed or unstressed, and properties like anaphoricity are not peculiar to one class. The one claim which has not yet been challenged concerning such questions is the claim that pronouns (or "anaphoric elements" generally) are stressed only in cases of "contrastive stress." As will be shown in the next section, however, contrastive stress does not appear to be a clearly definable notion.

THE STATUS OF CONTRASTIVE STRESS

While there have been numerous references to "contrastive stress" in the literature, as indicated in Chapter 3, there has been very little discussion concerning the nature of this entity. Two sorts of characterizations of contrastive stress have been implied in such references. One is what we may call the *phonetic* characterization, in which it is implied that contrastive stress is recognizable by purely phonetic properties. Such a characterization seems to be what Postal had in mind when he wrote: "... even for the class of morphological pronouns which Dougherty [1969] explicitly mentions, there are literally dozens of different types for which [his anaporn] relation fails, that is, dozens of contexts in which such pronouns have only stipulated coreferential readings. Below is a random selection of two dozen and two that obtain for my idiolect at least. I shall italicize the pronouns which are necessarily anaphoric. Since the stress level of pronouns is relevant, I distinguish v́ (contrastive stress), v̀ (strong but non-contrastive stress), v̆ (weak)" (1972:356). Such a characterization seems to be assumed in several of the passages cited in Chapter 3 as well, and in any work which refers to items which are "contrastively stressed."

The other characterization of contrastive stress which one finds implied in many works is a *semantic* characterization: here the assumption seems to be that contrastive stress is not distinguishable from primary stress phonetically but that it is assigned by some special rule(s). Thus the linguist can identify it by the meaning that is associated with it.[5] Lakoff, for example, implies such a semantic characterization in the following passage:

> Pronouns may, obviously enough, occur stressed under a number of conditions, such as deictic use, contrast etc.:
>
> (33)a. Helen detests thém. [pointing]
>   b. Hélen detests Hárry, and hé detests hér. [contrast]
> (1972:291)

The question which must be asked now, of course, is which of these characterizations, if either, is correct. The possibility of a phonetic characterization of the sort implied in the passage from Postal cited above was explicitly denied by Trager and Smith:

As for "contrastive stress," the facts are that when emphasis is desired on any part of an utterance, several procedures can be used. First, the primary stress can be put on any part of a phonemic phrase: compare . . . *How do they stúdy* . . . and *How do théy study* . . . one could also say *How dó they study* . . . Secondly, when one wishes to emphasize the item that already has primary stress, one can raise the pitch from /³/ to /⁴/ . . . Third, the low pitch as on *then* in [/³ hǽw+də+ðèy+stə̂diy¹#¹ðén#/] is a kind of emphasis. Fourth, one can contrast two items by having /³/ on the principal one, /²/ on the other, or, with greater emphasis /⁴/ and /³/: *I said ³Joe, not ²Bill* or *I said ⁴Joe, not ³Bill*; the contrast is in pitch, of course, not stress (and there are other ways of saying these sentences). Fifth, one can say the whole utterance, or certain parts of it, with greatly increased loudness and accompanying extra high, or, in some cases, extra low, pitch: this is often represented by special typography: *I said JOE, not Bill*. When this happens, the whole utterance or portion of it is stretched out horizontally and vertically, as it were . . . (1951:52)

Trager and Smith clearly imply that if the notion of "contrastive stress" is a viable one at all it is characterizable semantically (or "stylistically"). Phonetically (or phonemically) it is thus not one entity but a set of entities. What these entities have in common, it would appear, is that they deviate in some way from the "normal" pronunciation a sentence, or portion thereof, would receive. I suspect that this (transderivational) sort of characterization of contrastive stress is assumed by a number of linguists today, too; it is commonly stated, for example, that *trust* has contrastive stress in sentence (121):

(121) I'd give the money to Máry, but I don't trúst Mǎry.

Stockwell clearly has such a characterization in mind:

There is at least one type of example, observed first (so far as I know) by George Lakoff and called to my attention in this con-

nection by Mona Lindau, where the usual destressing of pronouns and other anaphoric elements is reversed: *Bill kicked
JOHN, and then HE kicked HIM*. This is necessary because of the
use of contrastive stress twice in the same sentence: *HE* referring to John in contrast to Bill, and *HIM* referring to Bill in contrast to John. Note that these can BE contrastive only by virtue
of the "normal" reading (for the same string in another context)
He KICKED him, where *he* is Bill and *him* is John. The notion
"contrastive stress" entails, as I see it, a prior notion of "non-
contrastive" or "normal" or "neutral" contours. (1971:44)

Thus this type of characterization (which is, of course, only as viable
as the notion of "normal stress") is still phonetic in a sense: while
the individual "contrastively stressed" items in a sentence are not
recognizable as such, the fact of their being "contrastively stressed"
is determinable by comparing the stress (or pitch) they receive with
the stress they receive in *other* utterances.

This possibility of characterizing contrastive stress is argued against
persuasively by Bolinger,[6] who observes:

> . . . we no sooner begin to contrast accents than we are tripped
> by the fact that one of the functions of accent is to MEAN con-
> trast, and in the act of performing the comparison we introduce
> one of the items to be compared. Suppose the utterance is *My
> mother is cóming*. The investigator wants to see what happens
> when the main accent occurs on prior words, so he tries it first
> on *is* (*My mother ís coming*), and concludes that this would im-
> ply a contrast with *is not*, then on *mother* (*My móther is com-
> ing*), and concludes that this would imply a contrast with *father*
> or *sister*, and then on *my* (*Mý mother is coming*), and concludes
> that this would imply a contrast with *your* or *his*. What is likely
> to escape him is that the contrastiveness of these accents is not
> only a function of the accents themselves but of the starting
> point. *My mother is cóming* already establishes a context in re-
> lation to which any other accent is contrastive. But if we fit the
> examples into a different context, for instance

> *Why are you in such a hurry to get home?*
> *My móther is coming.*

the accent on a prior word does not imply contrast. Similarly in

> *Why did you run?*
> *A políceman suddenly appeared around the corner.*

These are simply examples of the semantic peak occurring early in the utterance. The semantic peak includes contrastive accents along with other accents; and there is no predictable phonetic difference. In

> *How was the job?*
> *Oh, it was éasy.*
> *Was the job hard?*
> *No, it was éasy.*

the same pitch contour can be used in both answers. (1961*b*; in 1965:103)[7]

   If contrastive stress cannot be characterized phonetically (and I find Bolinger's argument that it cannot be thoroughly convincing), then the question remains of whether a semantic characterization is still possible. It should be clear that no such characterization can be found which will cover all the cases which have been called contrastive stress in the literature: as I have attempted to show in this section, the term has been used in several different ways by different linguists. Nevertheless we can still ask if there is some entity which we can refer to as contrastive stress, once it is understood that this would indicate something characterized semantically and not phonetically. It seems intuitively that there might be and, further, that the type of sentence given in (125) above would be an example of it and that the type given in (121) would not be.
   I shall discuss this question by way of a personal anecdote. In an earlier article (Schmerling 1971*b*) I discussed the problem of finding a usable criterion for identifying a given adjective-noun sequence as a

compound and stated, with reference to the possibility of relative-clause paraphrases: "This is one conceivable criterion for compound-ness, but it is not infallible. Examples like *whíte màn* and *óld pèople* are paraphrasable by *man who is white, people who are old*. Further-more, there are no corresponding NP analogous to *blâck bóard*; *whíte mán* and *ôld péople* are possible only in contrastive contexts" (1971*b*:65, n. 6). What I had in mind as an example where the last-mentioned phrases might appear was something like the following:

> (126) My candidate for president is a blâck wóman (and not a whîte mán).

—a sentence which might be described as contrasting both race and sex. What soon made me regret including this footnote in the article was my realization that it was hard to see how *blâck wóman* and *whíte mán* in the above sentence were any more "contrastive" than *blâck bóard* in a sentence like:

> (127) The hammer is over there on top of that blâck bóard.

The difference between the two seems to be this: in any context (in present-day America) where a sentence like (126) might be uttered, *man* would be the *only* thing with which *woman* could contrast. In an example like (127), on the other hand, *board* is potentially in con-trast with any physical object. It seems clear that this difference is merely one of degree. There is a sense in which anything meaningful is contrastive (in fact, one traditional definition of "meaningfulness" involves lack of total predictability in context), and the either/or kind of contrast with which we usually associate "contrastive stress" is but the limiting case.

The same point is made by Bolinger:

> No less troublesome than our inability to find a uniquely con-trastive pitch, however, is our failure to define what is meant by *contrastive*. Practically always the samples cited imply "*A* rather than *B*." But when we try to pin this down we find that the "ratherness" fades out gradually. In

> *I found a book.*
> *Whóse book?*
> *Jóhn's book.*
> *Not Jóe's?*

there is no difference between *whose*, *John's*, and *Joe's* as far as accent or reasons for accent are concerned, but we are likely to limit the term *contrastive* to the word *Joe's* in the last sentence of the series. In a broad sense every semantic peak is contrastive. Clearly in *Let's have a pícnic*, coming as a suggestion out of the blue, there is no specific contrast with *dinner party*, but there is a contrast between picnicking and anything else the group might do. As the alternatives are narrowed down, we get closer to what we think of as contrastive accent:

> *Where'll we have it?*
> *Let's have it in the párk.*
> *Can we all go?*
> *No, Jóhn can't.*
> *Bring some wíeners.*
> *I don't like wieners. I want hámburgers.* (1961*b*; reprinted

in 1965:106)

These observations suggest, then, that the notion of "contrastive stress," like the notion of "normal stress", is not a particularly useful one; contrastive stress does not seem to be a clearly definable entity unto itself.

The implications of this fact should be clear. If "contrastive stress" is not a definable entity, then we cannot attach any significance to claims that anaphoric items are unstressed except when contrastive stress is involved. This would suggest that the often-suggested correlation between stressability and anaphoricity does not exist.

A GENERALIZATION CONCERNING STRESSABILITY

The examples discussed above suggested that anaphoricity is neither a necessary nor a sufficient condition for a nominal to be unstressed.

We will now investigate this suggestion in more detail with the aim of discovering what sort of principle does seem to be involved.

The following pair of examples was discussed in Chapter 3:

(116) This is the mǎn I was télling you about.
(118) This is the mán I was telling you about.

As suggested in that chapter, the stress difference here correlates in an interesting way with the contexts in which these two sentences might be uttered, with (118) but not (116) being uttered in a context where the presence of a man is for some reason remarkable. Exactly the same kind of contrast can be found with examples involving nouns which are more "contentful":

(119) This is the dǒctor I was télling you about.
(117) This is the dóctor I was telling you about.

Thus (119) might well be uttered during a conversation between two hospital employees, in the hospital, or perhaps by a delegate at a medical convention, while we would expect (117) in more "normal" contexts where the presence of a doctor would be remarkable. As indicated in Chapter 3, it is not necessary for the speaker of (116) or (119) to assume that the addressee actually *knows* that the person in question is a man or a doctor; rather, the speaker must be able to assume that the addressee would not find the information that the individual in question was a man or a doctor to be particularly noteworthy. As a further example of this fact, consider the following hypothetical situation: I am visiting a relatively unfamiliar city and wish to go to a certain place by bus. I notice a bus stop a few feet away and ask a man walking near me if the bus that stops there can take me where I want to go. The man isn't sure but points to a woman who is standing by the bus stop and says:

(128) That woman thére might be able to tell you.

Suppose now that I am in a situation which is identical except that both a man and a woman are standing by the bus stop. Suppose further that the man has some feature which suggests to my informant that he would not be likely to be able to answer my question. In this case he would probably tell me:

(129) That wóman thére might be able to tell you.

In the case of sentence (128), the fact that the person in question is a woman is irrelevant, but this is not true in the case of (129), where the speaker intends to use the sex of the person as a means of identification. Thus, in (129) but not (128) the fact that the person in question is a woman is important to the assertion.

We can see the same effect in still another context. In uttering (128), the speaker could assume that the woman he was pointing to might be able to answer my question because she could reasonably be expected to be familiar with the bus line, not because she was a woman. Similarly, in (129) the woman could be expected to be able to answer the question for the same reason; the speaker singled her out because he had some reason to believe that the other person standing there would *not* be able to. Suppose now, however, that I am in a city where the culture of the inhabitants is such that only women are likely to be familiar with bus routes. Suppose further that this time I see no bus stop nearby and ask a man walking near me where I can catch the relevant bus. My informant sees a woman standing at the corner and utters (129). In this case the sex of the person is again relevant, but for a different reason: the speaker is assuming that she is likely to be able to help me *because* she is a woman. As with the previous situation, however, the fact that she is a woman is *for some reason* important to the assertion.

I have discussed this third, somewhat fanciful, context to point out that, while the term *contrastive stress* might have seemed plausible enough to describe the stress used in the second context (where, it seems, *that woman* "contrasts" with *that man*), it is not the term one is most likely to think of in describing the stress in the third context, where the idea of "contrast" seems less transparent. Yet the second and the third contexts show the same stress facts and a similar importance given to the sex of the person in question; it is only the *reason* for the importance that differs in the two cases.

The same sort of contrast can be found in nominals which are "nonreferential." Thus consider (130) and (131), two sentences which might be uttered in contemporary America:

> (130) Our department is looking for a mǎn who can teach mathematical linguístics.
> (131) Our department is looking for a wóman who can teach mathematical linguístics.

Sentence (131) might well be uttered by a department chairman who has a guilty conscience or who is under pressure from HEW; the sex of the candidate is of just as much importance as an ability to teach mathematical linguistics. Sentence (130), on the other hand, does not convey an analogous importance as regards the sex of the candidate: in this case, the speaker is announcing a desire to find a candidate who can teach mathematical linguistics and simply assuming that such a candidate would be a man; here the sex of the candidate is not important to the assertion. This difference would be reflected in possible continuations of the discourses where such sentences would be uttered. Suppose that an irate unemployed male mathematical linguist replied to (131) as in (132):

> (132) What about a mán who can teach mathematical linguistics?

(Here, of course, the sex of the candidate is important to the question and *man* is stressed.) Our department chairman could not give a reply like (133):

> (133) Well, yes, of course we'd consider men too.

without conveying the impression that he had suddenly changed his mind about the prerequisites for the position. Suppose, on the other hand, that an irate unemployed female mathematical linguist replied to (130) as in (134):

(134) What about a wóman who can teach mathematical linguis-
     tics?

In this case the chairman could reply as in (135):

(135) Well, yes, of course we'd consider women too.

He would probably come off sounding embarrassed but not inconsistent.[8]

The preceding examples show clearly that it is not semantic properties of nouns that are directly correlated with their stressability but
whether or not they denote something important to the content of
what is being uttered. If it is true, as has been suggested, that relatively "contentless" nouns like *man, woman, person* are "more likely"
to be unstressed than nouns with more content, then this is surely
due to facts about the world. (But I have no reason to assume that
this suggestion is true, let alone relevant.)

Quite similar observations can be made concerning another class of
nonanaphoric nominals, indefinite pronouns. As has often been noted, such pronouns frequently appear unstressed, as in (136) and
(137):

(136) It never occurred to me that sŏmething like thát would
     happen.
(137) I didn't tell ănyone where I was góing.

Examples such as these have been used to justify the claim that indefinite pronouns are one of those categories which are not assigned
stress.[9] Once again, however, it is not true that indefinite pronouns
cannot be stressed. Note (123) and (138):[10]

(123) There must be sómeone who can figure out what to do.
(138) Things are getting more and more suspicious-looking
     when he won't let ányone have access to the tapes.

There is an interesting difference between these pairs of examples
which emerges when one considers possible paraphrases of them.

Thus, consider (139) and (140) as paraphrase candidates for (136) and (123) respectively:

(139) It never occurred to me that at least one thing like thát would happen.

(140) There must be at least óne person who can figure out what to do.

Example (140) fares quite well as a paraphrase for (123), but (139), as a sentence of ordinary English rather than Logicianese, is ludicrous. It thus appears to be the case that the quantifiers embodied in the indefinite pronouns are an important part of the assertion in those cases where the indefinite pronouns are stressed, but not in the other cases.[11]

The examples discussed so far in this section show clearly that anaphoricity is not a necessary condition for a nominal to fail to be stressed. As should already be obvious, it is not a sufficient condition either, though indeed anaphoric items frequently are unstressed, as in the examples in (141):

(141) I'd give the money to Jóhn, but I don't trúst
$$\begin{Bmatrix} \text{hĭm} \\ \text{the băstard} \\ \text{the măn} \\ \text{Jŏhn} \end{Bmatrix}.$$

While the different unstressed items in (141) differ morphologically, and while, as Lakoff (1968) has shown, they cannot all be used in the same contexts, they agree in failing to be stressed. That anaphoricity cannot be invoked as the *reason* for their failure to be stressed, however, is clear from the fact that anaphoric items may indeed be stressed, as in (142):

(142) I know who's standing in front of Máry, but I don't know
who $\begin{Bmatrix} \text{Máry's} \\ \text{shé's} \end{Bmatrix}$ in front of.[12]

Or, to give a more famous example, consider the following, due to Lakoff 1971*b*:

(143) Jôhn insulted Máry, and then shê insŭlted hím.[13]

While (142) and (143) would frequently be referred to as examples of "contrastive stress," we saw earlier that the impossibility of giving a precise characterization to this notion means that we cannot simply so label such examples and dismiss them.

Looking at (142) and (143), we see that an important part of these assertions involves the "newness" of the semantic relations involved in the second conjuncts: in (143), for example, insulting is constant in the two conjuncts; what is "new" in the second conjunct is neither insulting nor the characters involved but the semantic *relations* involved. A similar case is given in (144):

(144) Jôhn insulted Máry, and then Sâlly insulted Fréd.

Just as in (143), the semantic relations in the second conjunct are new. The difference between (143) and (144)—that a new cast of characters is involved in the second conjunct of (144)—does not seem to have any bearing on the question of what items get stressed; it is the newness of the semantic relations that is significant. In other words, an important part of these assertions involves filling in the x and y slots in x *insulted* y; it does not matter if the referents of these nouns have been mentioned previously or not.

This is not to say that nominals will be stressed whenever the semantic relations are new; this is not the case, as shown by example (145):

(145) Jôhn insulted Máry, and then shĕ slápped hǐm.

But the *difference* in semantic relations is not the main point of the assertion here, as it is in (143).

The fact that the importance or lack thereof of a difference in semantic relations is crucial in the assignment of stress to nominals is reflected in several of the examples in a well-known squib by Akmajian and Jackendoff (1970), and is probably illustrated most nicely in the following pair of sentences:

(146) John hit Bill and then George hit him. (*him* is *Bill*) (=Akmajian and Jackendoff's [11])

(147) John hit Bill and then George hit *him*. (*him* is *John*) (=Akmajian and Jackendoff's [12])

The crucial difference between these two examples lies in the direct-object relation of the second conjunct in each case: in (146) the direct object in the second conjunct is the same as that in the first conjunct—hence the lack of stress on *him*. In (147), on the other hand, the difference between the direct objects in the two conjuncts is an important part of what is being asserted. Akmajian and Jackendoff, of course, suggested that sentences such as these provided evidence for a direct correlation between stress level and "interpretation of coreferentiality"; the observations in this chapter would suggest that this correlation follows from a more general phenomenon.[14]

We have thus seen that it is not anaphoricity that is directly correlated with lack of stress but, rather, lack of "significance" in some sense. Intuitively, the generalization appears to be that certain items in an utterance may be "taken for granted" and thus eliminated from consideration, as it were, in stress assignment. Exactly the same observation can be made for cases of identity-of-sense anaphora. Thus, consider (143) again:

(143) Jôhn insulted Máry, and then shê insŭlted hím.

As indicated above, insulting is constant in the two conjuncts in this example and, what is relevant for our purposes here, *insulted* is not stressed in the second conjunct. As with the cases of identity-of-reference anaphora, however, it can be seen quite easily that an item's being anaphoric in this latter sense is neither a necessary nor a sufficient condition for it to be unstressed. As one example showing that it is not a necessary condition, consider (148), due again to Lakoff 1971*b*:

(148) Jôhn càlled Mâry a Repúblican, and then shê insǔlted hím.

As Lakoff notes, this sentence is quite possible if the speaker holds a belief that to be called a Republican is an insult.[15] Thus, in this sentence, *insulted* is not anaphoric in a strict sense; yet, given the relevant speaker belief, it is entailed by the material in the first conjunct. Thus in this case it is "taken for granted," just like material which is, strictly speaking, anaphoric. Numerous interesting examples of this kind of entailment are found in Green 1968.

Another example, not involving identity-of-sense anaphora, is given in (149). Suppose a colleague and I are discussing English syntax in my office when we hear a female scream from the next office. Suppose further that we know that Harry, the inhabitant of this office, has a reputation for getting too friendly with his female students. Given this background I could say:

(149) Who's Hǎrry trẙing to sedǔce thís time?

Clearly, the sequence *Harry trying to seduce* in this sentence is not anaphoric; yet it is, in a sense, taken for granted and not stressed.

We have seen, then, that anaphoricity fails to be a necessary condition for lack of stress in cases involving this type of anaphora as well. Not surprisingly, it turns out that it is not a sufficient condition either. Thus consider the following exchange:

(150) Speaker A: They sure don't have ridiculous constructions like this in Tübatulabal.

Speaker B: Do you know Tübatulabal?

Speaker A: Some.

Speaker B: Wow, if yôu knòw Tübatulabál, maybe you can tell me something I've always been wondering about.

The interesting part of this dialogue for our purposes is the *if* clause of the last sentence. Clearly the material in this clause is anaphoric, in the relevant sense; yet it is not unstressed. Clearly, too, as the antecedent of a conditional it is an important part of the assertion; in uttering this sentence the speaker does not treat this material as "taken for granted" even though it is "old information."

To conclude this section, then, we have seen that there is a generalization concerning stressability of items in an utterance which can be stated roughly and intuitively as in (I):

> (I) Certain items in an utterance are treated by the speaker as relatively "insignificant" and fail to be assigned stress.

It is thus the thesis of this chapter that the question of what relative stress levels are assigned items in a given utterance arises in the case of those items which are not eliminated from consideration by a principle like (I). That is, material which is not so eliminated from consideration is subject to various rules governing the assignment of relative stress levels; such rules will be discussed in Chapter 5.

For the present, then, the problem we are faced with is that of clarifying principle (I). As we shall see in the next section, this is a task which no current theory is up to.

THEORETICAL IMPLICATIONS OF THE GENERALIZATION

Speaker assumptions have been the subject of a great number of linguistics articles in recent years, and a variety of types of assumption seem to be correlated with various formal properties (lexical, syntactic, morphological, and phonological) of utterances. Of all the phenomena which could be included here, the one which has received the most attention is presupposition, a term which has itself been used to refer to phenomena which should probably be kept distinct. Yet, despite the large amount of work done both on the relationships between presuppositions and formal properties of utterances and on what Langendoen and Savin (1971) called the "projection problem" of presuppositions (on which see also Morgan 1969*b*; 1973; Karttunen 1973; 1974), there is still no solidly established analysis of how such facts are to be represented, or of the nature of presupposition itself.[16]

Despite the fact that the one solidly established conclusion concerning presupposition is that it is not well understood, a number of authors, myself included, have assumed in the past that this notion is intimately bound up with questions concerning stress. Chomsky, for example, argues that a semantically significant aspect of utterances is what he calls *focus*, which on his account is a constituent in surface structure which includes the primary stress of the sentence; he uses the term *presupposition* for what is obtained by replacing the "focus" with a "variable" (1970*a*). (For example, on Chomsky's account, the focus of *Jôhn hìt Bíll* could be *Bill*, in which case the presupposition would be *John hit someone*.) Chomsky's account of the facts is challenged in Schmerling 1971*a*, where I argued for the existence of the following principle:

> Those portions of sentences receive reduced stress which contain material presupposed by the speaker to be true and to be known to the addressee(s).

(It was and is my contention that if *John hit someone* is "presupposed," the sentence in question will be pronounced *Jôhn hìt Bíll*.[17]) It seems clear, however, that it is wrong to identify what I have called "taken-for-granted" material in an utterance with what have been called presuppositions by other writers.

Consider, for example, sentences with so-called factive predicates, which, on the account given in Kiparsky and Kiparsky 1970 and many subsequent works, presuppose the truth of their complements. One such factive predicate is *realize*; on the usual account of factivity, sentence (151) presupposes that it was raining:

(151) I didn't realize it was raining.

(On a pragmatic account of presupposition, the *speaker* of (151) presupposes that it was raining. On either a semantic or pragmatic account, however, the proposition that it was raining is said to be presupposed true, and this is what is of importance to the present discussion.) As I argued in Schmerling 1971a, however, whether or not this complement sentence is stressed depends on other factors. In a context like that given in (152), where the speaker assumes that the addressee already knows that it was raining, the complement will be unstressed:

> (152) Speaker A: If it was raining, why on earth didn't you take your umbrella?
>
> Speaker B: Because I was so distraught I didn't réalize ĭt wăs răining.

In a context like that given in (153), on the other hand, the speaker does not make this assumption and the complement of *realize* is stressed:

> (153) I managed to get totally drenched this morning. When I went outside, I didn't realize it was ráining.

It was facts such as these which led me to include the second conjunct in the condition for lack of stress given in the principle quoted above. But presupposition has nothing to do with these facts. We can see this by comparing examples involving nonfactive predicates, which show exactly the same behavior with respect to stress:

> (154) Speaker A: I thought John was coming, but I don't see him anywhere.
>
> Speaker B: Well, he sáid hĕ wăs cŏming, but you know how reliable he is.

> (155) Speaker A: Where's John?
>
> Speaker B: I don't know. He said he was cóming, but I haven't seen him.

It thus seems clear that the distinction between what is "taken for granted" and what is not cross-cuts the distinction between what is and what is not presupposed, given the usual use of the term *presupposition*.

Numerous other examples could be given showing that the usual notion of presupposition, whether this is taken to be a semantic or a pragmatic notion, is distinct from the notion under discussion here. Thus, consider a sentence discussed earlier in this chapter:

(116) This is the măn I was télling you about.

It might seem at first glance plausible to maintain that the proposition *x is a man* is presupposed in this sentence, but such a suggestion will not stand up to any scrutiny. As indicated earlier, it is not necessary for the speaker of such a sentence to assume that his audience already knows that the person in question is a man. It is rather that the fact that he is a man is unimportant to the assertion as a whole. Such a suggestion is valid only if one intends the term *presupposition* to be taken in a new sense.

An even worse problem shows up in the fact that *telling* in this example *is* stressed, since, under either a semantic or a pragmatic account of presupposition, it is reasonable to claim that restrictive relative clauses are presupposed true.[18] On the other hand, the content of the relative clause is important to this sentence: it is identifying the person in question.[19]

It thus seems clear that, whatever we call the kind of assumption which is involved in principle (I), it is wrong to identify it with other phenomena which have been called presuppositions. This is a phenomenon of a fundamentally different nature, one which linguists have not even begun to deal with.

Another sort of distinction which has been mentioned in the literature from time to time is that between "old information" and "new information," and one might want to suggest that it is this distinction which is relevant to the phenomena in this chapter.[20] Yet it can also be shown that this is not the relevant distinction, taking these terms to mean what they suggest intuitively. Thus, in (116), for example, the fact that the person in question is a man need not be old information; this information can very well be new, but not significant to the assertion as a whole. On the other hand, old information may be stressed if it is a significant part of what is being asserted; the following are examples of this sort of case:

(143) Jôhn insulted Máry, and then shê insülted hím.
(156) Wow, if yôu knòw Tübatulabál, maybe you can tell me something I've always been wondering about.

Examples like (143) point up an additional problem for the phenomenon under discussion. Previous discussions concerning facts such as these have assumed that it is possible to divide an utterance neatly into "old information" and "new information," or a "presupposed part" and a "nonpresupposed part" or "focus." Yet consider *she* and *him* in (143). These in a sense correspond to "old information" or "presupposed material." Yet in another sense they correspond to new material, namely, new semantic relations, and, as we have seen, it is this fact which seems to be relevant to the fact that they are stressed. It is thus an unfortunate fact that items in the surface structure of an utterance do not "correspond" in a direct way to particular aspects of a "logical structure"; examples like this point up this problem very painfully, and no theory I am aware of has come to grips with it.

Thus the facts presented in this chapter show clearly that we are far from having an adequate theory of semantic representation and its relation to the surface form of utterances. They also show that any theory which purports to be a model of the linguistic competence of a native speaker must have a way of stating pragmatic principles like (I). We do not yet have such a theory.

Despite the problems involved in stating precisely the principles involved in determining which items in an utterance fail to receive stress, the thesis of this chapter should be clear. Certain items in an utterance may be treated as "insignificant" or "taken for granted" and are not stressed. Whether or not they are so treated has no direct correlation with grammatical properties like category membership;

there is a direct correlation between stress and pragmatic factors. Descriptions of English stress which ignore this fact are forced to make either false or empirically vacuous claims.

5 Relative Stress Levels

      As was shown in Chapter 4, certain items in an utterance, which are treated as "insignificant" in terms of the information they convey, are not stressed. This chapter will deal with those items in an utterance which *are* assigned stress. In the assignment of stress, rather than one principle like the NSR being involved, several different principles exist which interact with each other. Because of this interaction it is impossible to discuss each of these principles in isolation, and I will therefore discuss them in the order which seems most convenient for purposes of exposition. While no claim is intended here that the principles to be discussed account for all aspects of English sentence stress, these principles, taken together, do go a long way in accounting for various stress patterns, without the necessity for ad hoc devices of the sort discussed in Chapter 1, which would be needed to make the NSR "work." The principles fall into two distinct classes: pragmatically based principles referring to discourse function, and phonological principles related to phrasing and tempo.

LOWER STRESSING OF PREDICATES

As noted in Chapter 1, an interesting generalization emerges when one notes the relative stress levels of nouns and verbs in simple sentences where the entire sentence is "news." Thus the stress on *John* and on *Bill* in (1) is greater than the stress on *hit*, and the stress on *John* is greater than the stress on *died* in (102):

    (1) Jôhn hìt Bíll.
  (102) Jôhn dîed.

I will refer to such sentences as these, where the speaker assumes no particular expectations with regard to the information content on the part of his audience, as simple "news sentences," for want of a better term.[1] The following generalization emerges when one looks at such sentences:

(II) The verb receives lower stress than the subject and the direct object, if there is one; in other words, predicates receive lower stress than their arguments, irrespective of their linear position in surface structure.

An approach like Chomsky and Halle's must treat this fact as an accident, since, as discussed above, primary stress must be assigned to *John* in (102) by a different rule from the one which has the effect of assigning greater stress to *John* and *Bill* in (1).[2] The approach taken here, on the other hand, is to treat this fact as a linguistically significant generalization which should be expressed directly in the grammar. In other words, I am suggesting that there is a rule of English which says, in effect, "Put lower stress on predicates than on their arguments." Such a rule will not, of course, account for the greater stress on *Bill* than on *John* in (1). As we shall see in the next section, however, this latter fact is itself explained by another very general principle of the sort suggested by Newman, which *does* depend crucially on the linear position of items in surface structure. The generality of Newman's principle is, in fact, one argument for the existence of a principle which says only that *John* and *Bill* in this example should be heavily stressed relative to the verb.

Because of the paucity of movement rules in English which would bear on the claims concerning the existence of a rule of the sort I am proposing here, it is hard to find direct evidence one way or the other. (That is, the applicability of a rule like Topicalization, for example, seems to be correlated with certain assumptions on the part of the speaker, and thus we would expect that the stress contour of a sentence in which such a rule applies might not necessarily correspond in a direct way to the stress contour of a "corresponding" sentence in which this rule does not apply.) One such rule which does bear on this issue, however, is Particle Movement, which relates sentences (58) and (157):

(58) I lôoked ùp the ánswer.
(157) I lôoked the ánswer ûp.

The failure of *up* to receive a primary stress in (157) might be thought at first to be due to an inability of particles to take primary stress.[3] However, an approach which tries to account for (157) on the basis of such a claim will not work, as this claim concerning stress level of particles is false. When the direct object in such a sentence is itself unstressed, the particle does indeed receive a primary stress, as in (158):

(158) I lôoked it úp.

Thus an approach which attempts to account for (157) on the basis of a claim that the relevant stress rule(s) cannot apply to particles is doomed to failure. On the other hand, the rule I am proposing in this section predicts the facts in (157), since it predicts that, in this case, *answer* must receive greater stress than *look* and *up*. Furthermore, taken together with the other principles to be discussed in this chapter, it contributes toward an account of the stress contours in all the examples cited here. The tertiary stress on *up* in (58) is accounted for by the rhythm rule to be discussed in the fourth section (evidence for the existence of which was presented in Ch. 1), while the primary stress on *up* in (158) is accounted for by the principle of Newman's to be discussed in the next section.

Some slight evidence for the existence of the rule I am arguing for in this section is provided by proverbs with abnormal word order. Thus, for example, *acorns* receives a primary stress in both (159) and (160):

(159) Great oaks from little ácorns grow.
(160) Great oaks grow from little ácorns.

Examples like these would seem to indicate that, in this case, the primary stress on *acorns* in (160) is not due to its final position in surface structure.[4]

By far the most compelling argument for the existence of a rule like the one I am proposing here—a rule which does not depend on the linear position of elements in surface structure—comes, in my opinion, from extralinguistic evidence, evidence concerning the behavior of English-speakers learning German. Note that the stress levels on the different words are the same in (161) and (162):

    (161) Ich sah Háns.
         I   saw Hans. 'I saw Hans.'

    (162) weil   ich Háns sah
         because I   Hans saw 'because I saw Hans'

If something like the *SPE* approach to English sentence stress is correct, German sentence stress must be governed by quite different
principles,[5] and English-speakers should have difficulty learning
them; specifically, they should have difficulty learning that the primary stress does not fall on *sah* in (162). Contrary to this expectation, however, this is not the case: while English-speakers do encounter difficulty with the correct word order, the stress seems to cause
no problems. That is, once the English-speaker masters the correct
order, the correct stress comes automatically.[6] The principle I am arguing for in this section would explain why this is so: the same principle is at work in English and German, and English-speakers learning
German do not have to learn a new principle, radically different from
any in English. Notice, in fact, what happens when English-speakers
talk about German; one often hears statements like the following:

    (163) In German you can't say "Because I saw Háns"; you have
         to say "Because I Háns saw."

Once again, a principle which says that the primary stress goes on
Hans in this English expression because of its linear position in surface structure would predict that a speaker talking about German
word order would talk about saying "because I Hans sáw" and *not*
"because I Háns saw."
    The facts concerning English-speakers learning German contrast
markedly with the facts concerning English-speakers learning French,
a language which is very different from English in terms of suprasegmentals. It has frequently been noted that prosodic features provide
one of the most serious phonological difficulties for an English-
speaker learning French. This is, of course, what we would predict if,

in fact, the two languages differ in this regard. The fact that a treatment of English stress along the lines suggested in *SPE* forces us to claim that different principles are involved in English and German stress, then, forces us to predict that English speakers should have a comparable difficulty with German. Thus this sort of treatment forces us to say that English and German are different in a way in which they appear in fact not to be.

Notice that I am *not* claiming here that English must have a particular stress rule because German seems to have such a rule. I am claiming rather that any analysis of the two languages which claims that they are different in this regard makes wrong predictions concerning what a native speaker of one language will have to learn is different about the other. I am thus making crucial use of the assumption that the rules in question are intended by the analyst to have some psychological reality. A framework which holds that the rules linguists write to account for such phenomena are merely descriptions of the data and can therefore be regarded as convenient fictions will not, of course, be making any claims concerning what will happen when a speaker of one language learns another, and it is, of course, perfectly possible to interpret the *SPE* stress rules in such a way. Such an interpretation is not, however, the interpretation the authors of *SPE* themselves give to their rules, and thus in arguing against the *SPE* approach and for the particular principle I am presenting in this section I am maintaining the position taken by Chomsky and Halle that the rules a linguist writes ought to reflect a psychological reality. Linguists who maintain such a position will not want their analyses to claim that two languages differ in a particular respect if in fact they seem not to so differ.[7]

NEWMAN'S NUCLEAR HEAVY STRESS PRINCIPLE

In this section I will consider a stress-assignment principle which is quite similar to Newman's treatment of what he considered to be allophonic variation among stresses which he assigned to his heavy stress phoneme (see Ch. 1). It will be recalled that Newman's principle was that the rightmost "heavy stress" in an "intonational unit" was heavier than the others and bore the melodic contour characteristic of the type of "intonational unit" of which it was the "nucleus." As indicated in Chapter 1, it is obvious from Newman's discussion that he conceived of his "intonational units" as being defined intonationally and not syntactically; they are thus equivalent not to syntactic constituents but to what linguists would refer to today as "phonological phrases" or "breath-groups." In the present discussion I will not be concerned with the problem of defining these entities; I will instead limit my discussion to examples which consist of only one such unit. I will thus be arguing for the following principle, which holds within such a unit:

(III) Given a sequence of stresses which are equal and greater than other stresses within the intonational unit, the last such stress will be more prominent than the others.

The interaction of this principle and principle (II), discussed in the preceding section, should already be clear. As indicated above, principle (II) will assign greater stress to *John* and *Bill* than to *hit* in a sentence like (1). We can thus think of an intermediate stage in the assignment of stress to this sentence as something like that indicated in (164):

(164) Jóhn hît Bíll.

At this level of representation *John* and *Bill* have equal stress, and these stresses are the heaviest stresses in the sentence. Principle (III) will thus assign greater prominence to *Bill*.

It is being claimed here that greater prominence is assigned to *Bill* in this sentence by a principle which is quite different from the principle which says that *John* and *Bill* are themselves more prominent than *hit*. The crucial point of the last section was that this latter principle was one which assigned lower stress to predicates than to their arguments, irrespective of their position in surface structure. Principle (III), on the other hand, refers crucially to surface-structure position and is a "superficial" principle in the sense that other principles are logically prior to it. What must be emphasized at this point is that (III) is in no way an ad hoc principle needed to patch up the output of a previous rule. It is, on the contrary, a very general principle, the effects of which show up elsewhere.

Another area in which the effect of (III) can be seen involves sentences with coordinate constituents, which, as shown in Chapter 1, provide a severe problem for the *SPE* analysis of stress. Consider the following sentences:

(25) Jôhn and Bîll hìt Hárry.
(26) Jôhn wàshed and drìed the díshes.
(165) Hĕ wâshed and dríed thĕm.
(166) Jôhn and Bíll are còming.
(27) Jôhn hìt Bîll and Hárry.

Contrary to the predictions made by the cyclic approach of *SPE*, which predicts that the rightmost conjunct in any such constituent will receive greater stress than those to the left, we see that the rightmost conjunct receives greater stress only if it will thus have the heaviest stress of the sentence. This is exactly what is predicted by (III) and what is in no way predicted by a cyclic approach to stress. To see how (III) works here, note the examples below, which can, again, be thought of as intermediate representations produced by the principle discussed in the previous section:

(167) Jóhn and Bíll hît Hárry.
(168) Jóhn wâshed and drîed the díshes.
(169) Hĕ wáshed and dríed thĕm.
(170) Jóhn and Bíll are côming.
(171) Jóhn hît Bíll and Hárry.

Principle (III) will now assign greatest prominence to the rightmost in each of these sentences, thus producing the correct contours.

A third area where we can see the effects of (III) is in the verb-particle constructions discussed above; as has been shown, the particle will receive greater stress than the verb in such a construction only in cases where it has the greatest stress of the sentence (or intonational unit). Another example of a verb-particle construction where (III) operates is example (172):

(172) What did you have to lôok úp?

This sort of example contrasts with a superficially similar example ending with a verb plus a preposition:

(173) What did you have to sít òn?

As indicated in Chapter 2, examples such as these would appear to provide counterexamples to Bresnan's claim (1971; 1972) that the stress contours assigned simple sentences are preserved in complex constructions, since verb-particle constructions and verb + prepositional-phrase constructions are not distinguished in terms of stress in simple sentences. Bresnan is thus forced to provide some ad hoc treatment of verb-particle cases. The facts concerning the stress in these constructions follow automatically from the non–ad hoc proposals presented here, however. It should be pointed out that I have not attempted at this point to account for stress on prepositions, an area which is beyond the scope of this work. It must be noted, however, that the facts concerning an example like (173) are in no way predicted to be otherwise by any of the principles I am arguing for here. Thus such an example indicates an area which has yet to be dealt with but provides no counterexample to anything which has been proposed here so far.

A fourth area where we can see the explanatory value of principle (III) involves certain adjective-noun sequences. Recall that the cyclic approach to stress predicts that the noun in such a case will always have a greater stress than the adjective. Once again, however, this seems to be the case only if the noun will thereby have the greatest stress of the sentence. Thus compare (174) and (175):

(174) He's a gôod mán.
(175) He's a gôod mân with a knífe.

On the assumption that the stress on *good* and *man* is predicted to be equal by some "deeper" principle here, the fact that *man* receives a primary stress in (174) but not (175) follows automatically from

(III). Examples (176) and (177) are also worthy of note here:

(176) You can't keep a gôod mân dówn.
(177) You can't keep a gôod màn dówn.

The difference between these two cases seems to be largely one of tempo, (177) being an example of a somewhat faster tempo than (176). It is thus another example of the application of the rhythm rule to be discussed below. The slower-timed (176) again shows a case where the stresses on adjective and noun are equal and where the noun does not have the greatest stress of the sentence. While the stresses on adjective-noun sequences deserve greater study, the point to note here is that cases like these provide further evidence for the great generality of (III).

TOPIC-COMMENT CASES

Principle (II)—that predicates receive lower stress than their arguments—is valid for simple news sentences—sentences which would be uttered by a speaker who is making no assumptions as to the expectations of his audience regarding the propositional content of the utterance. Clearly, however, there are cases where the verb receives the primary stress. Some of these cases involve subjects which fail to be stressed because they are "taken for granted"—cases of the sort discussed in Chapter 4—and where, from the point of view I am taking here, the verb in effect gets stressed by default. There are, however, numerous sentences in which both the subject and the predicate are stressed,[8] with slightly greater stress on the predicate. It is easy to construct a number of examples in which such a sentence contrasts with an otherwise identical sentence having the primary stress on the subject, and in which the first sentence appears to involve some special assumption on the part of the speaker which the second does not involve. Informants readily agree with these judgments, so it

is clear that the difference in question is rule-governed in some way—
the only alternative, that we are dealing with sentential idioms
learned complete with stress contour, clearly being untenable. I shall
discuss a number of such cases with the special assumptions they
seem to be correlated with and then attempt a characterization of
what the various examples have in common. As will be clear, I am
not able at this time to propose a specific treatment of these cases in
a grammar; but the discussion here is the requisite preliminary step
toward doing this.

As a first example of the type of contrast under discussion, we
may return to a pair of sentences discussed earlier:

> (92) Jóhnson dîed.
> (91) Trûman díed.

Sentences (92) and (91) represent the reports of the deaths of two
former presidents as I heard them and as, I assume, large numbers of
Americans heard them. The different stress contours seem to be correlated with differences in the contexts in which these two reports
were uttered. Johnson's death came out of the blue; it was not news
that we were waiting for. In other words, (92) is the type of simple
news sentence discussed in the first section of this chapter. When
Truman died, on the other hand, his condition had been the subject
of daily news reports for some time. Thus a speaker uttering (91)
could assume that the audience was aware of the possibility that this
report would in fact be given. This fact seems to correlate with another fact: (178) seems impossible as an out-of-the-blue report:

> (178) Jóhn survîved.
> (179) Jôhn survíved.

Such a report could be uttered only in a context where some such
expectation on the part of the audience was assumed by the speaker
(say, if we know that our friend John has been involved in a serious
automobile accident).

Let us now consider another such contrast, which does not seem
at first glance to be anything like the one given above, apart from the

stress contours involved. Note the different contexts in which sentences (180) and (181) might be uttered:

(180) The statue's héad is mîssing.
(181) The statue's hêad is míssing.

Example (180) is, again, a news sentence: it might be a report of vandalism, for example. Example (181), on the other hand, sounds like part of a description of the statue. It might thus be uttered by a guide in a museum who was trying to tell the addressee what the statue in question looked like so that the addressee could identify it. A similar contrast is involved in the following pair:

(182) His háir is lông.
(183) His hâir is lóng.

Sentence (182) might be uttered in a context like the following:

(184) They wouldn't let John into Disneyland because his háir is lông.

Sentence (183), on the other hand, sounds necessarily like part of a description. It thus might be uttered by someone who was describing a friend to an addressee who was supposed to meet this friend at the airport but did not know him.
    A third interesting contrast involves sentences like (185) and (186):

(185) I didn't have any trouble getting into the house because the dóor was ôpen.
(186) I didn't have any trouble getting into the house because the dôor was ópen.

Unlike the other pairs of examples discussed so far, the two sentences above seem equally appropriate; it is hard to see at first glance what difference there might be between them in terms of the contexts in which they might be uttered. Consider now, however, (187) and (188):

(187) I didn't have any trouble getting into the house because the front wíndow was ôpen.
(188) I didn't have any trouble getting into the house because the front wîndow was ópen.

Here, (187) seems to be a perfectly normal utterance, but (188) does not: it seems, unlike (187), to presuppose that it would have been the normal or expected thing for the speaker to enter the house through the front window. This fact seems to correlate with the fact that both (185) and (186) seem perfectly normal: it *is* normal to enter a house through the door.

A fourth interesting contrast is provided by sentences (189) and (190):

(189) I had a grây háir fâll ôut.
(190) I had a grây hâir fâll óut.

Sentence (190), but not (189), seems to presuppose that the speaker has numerous gray hairs. It sounds as if the speaker of this sentence is upset basically at the thought of one of these hairs falling out. Sentence (189), on the other hand, might be uttered by someone who was upset at discovering the presence of a gray hair; in this case the fact of the hair's falling out is of importance only insofar as it led to the discovery of this hair.

It is obvious that, in each of the cases discussed, the example with primary stress on the predicate seems to involve some special assumption on the part of the speaker which is not present in the cases where the subject receives primary stress. The problem now becomes one of discovering what these varied cases have in common.

The one approach I am aware of to describe differences such as those discussed here is that of Bolinger, discussed in Chapter 2. The type of account which Bolinger would give involves what he would refer to as the relative semantic weight of the subject and predicate: he would claim that in a context where the predicate was relatively "predictable" the subject would receive the primary stress (or "sentence accent," in his terms). As indicated in Chapter 2, this approach seems incapable of accounting for differences such as these; I will mention just two cases briefly here. Consider (91) and (92). Since Truman's failing health had been in the news for some time when he finally died, his death was in a sense predictable. On Bolinger's account, then, the mention of Truman in such a context should suggest "death," and therefore *died* should not receive the primary stress. On the other hand, the mention of Johnson at the time when he died should not have suggested "death" any more than anything else one might want to say about him, and therefore *died* should receive the primary stress in this sentence. Clearly, then, Bolinger's account would appear to predict stress contours opposite to the ones which actually occur in these cases. Consider, likewise, examples (187) and (188). Given the contexts represented in the first parts of these sentences, "open" should be equally predictable in the two cases. Yet *open* fails to receive a primary stress in only one of the cases. Additional examples pointing to the same problem are discussed in Chapter 2. It thus seems clear that an account in terms of relative "information" is unable to explain the cases under discussion.

What I would like to suggest here is that something like the notion of topic and comment is involved in the cases having primary stress on the predicate. These terms are unfortunate because of their notorious vagueness and because of the fact that different writers have probably used them in different ways, but I am unable at this time to suggest more felicitous terminology. What *I* mean by these terms is the following: the cases discussed here which have primary stress on the predicate all seem intuitively to be "about" the subject of the sentence rather than an entire event or state of affairs; that is, in uttering such a sentence, the speaker brings up some topic and says something about it—makes a comment. Consider (91) and (92). In (91), the speaker of the sentence brings up Truman, who has been the subject of all these news reports, and says something about him. The utterance in (92), concerning Johnson's death, is not organized in the same way: since Johnson has not been the subject of such reports, the speaker does not assume that he has been on the addressee's mind in the same way.

Consider now examples (180)–(183), in which the cases of predicate stress sound like parts of descriptions. If it is established that the speaker is going to describe the statue, for example, we can expect him to bring up various aspects of the statue's appearance and comment on them. A report of vandalism, which (180) could be, will not involve this sort of expectation. Such an expectation is likewise involved in the *door* and *window* cases. In the predicate-stressed cases the speaker is bringing up some means of entry to the house and commenting on it. When this is done with *door* the sentence does not sound at all strange; we *expect* the door to be this means of entry. It sounds strange to treat *window* in this way precisely because we do not expect the window to be a means of entry to the house, and consequently we would not expect the speaker to bring it up and comment on it as such. The subject-stressed cases sound perfectly natural whether *door* or *window* is involved because this element of expectation is not there.

What I am calling the *topic* in each of these cases is then a kind of "old information": it is something the speaker can assume to be, in a sense, on the addressee's mind, or immediately inferable from the total context. It is this fact which seems to be responsible for our reactions to the *gray hair* cases. In (190) the gray hair must in a sense be old information, and from this fact and the use of the indefinite article we can infer that the speaker is talking about only one of many gray hairs. Since *gray hair* in (189) need not be "old information," we do not necessarily infer that it is only one of many.

If these observations are correct, then the notions of topic and comment must be clarified and incorporated into linguistic theory, so that something like the following principle can be stated (or deduced) in this theory:[9]

> (IV) In a topic-comment utterance, stress both the topic and the comment.

The slightly heavier stress on the "comment" follows from principle (III).

There are two important issues for future research in this area which should be considered at this point. The first has to do with the question of what predicates function as comments. The attentive reader will note that I have discussed no cases of news sentences in which the predicate has the form of a noun phrase. It is indeed hard to find such cases; one such is given in (191):

(191) I didn't want to go because my háir was a mêss.

A mess does indeed have the form of a noun phrase, but, in the terminology of Ross 1972, it is not very "nouny," as can be seen from the following:

(192) I'll be along later; first I have an awful mess to clean up.
(193) I'll be along later; first I have this mess to clean up.
(194) *I'll be along later; first I have a mess to clean up.
(195) *I have three messes to clean up.

Most predicates which have the form of noun phrases describe what might be referred to as permanent properties of the subject; this is true of all of the following examples:

(196) She is a doctor.
(197) She is a hard worker.
(198) She is a member of the Communist Party.
(199) She is a Swede.
(200) She is a thoroughly obnoxious character.

Apparently, predicates which denote such properties appear only in what I am calling "topic-comment" utterances. The problem is this: it has been argued convincingly by Bach (1968) and others that there is no need to distinguish nouns, verbs, and adjectives in terms of semantic considerations: all function as predicates. Significant distinctions between types of predicates, such as the stative/nonstative distinction, are found in each of these syntactic classes (see Lakoff 1970*a* and Bach 1968 for discussion); in other words, the stative/nonstative distinction is not correlated with any morphosyntactic distinction among predicates. Nevertheless it seems to be the case that almost all (but not only) predicates which have the form of noun phrases are predicates denoting inherent attributes. The question which must be faced at this point is whether this is an accident or whether it points to a "deeper" significance to morphosyntactic distinctions among predicates than has previously been recognized— that is, whether a significant distinction exists between nouns and other predicates in terms of their function in discourse.

The second problem for future research involves the important question of the relationship between the "topic-comment"/"news" distinction and the syntax of these utterances. I know of no evidence that a pair of sentences like (91) and (92) differ syntactically in any way. It does seem to be the case, however, that the application of certain syntactic rules is somehow correlated with this distinction. One such rule is Topicalization. In the cases of the "topic-comment" utterances I have discussed so far the topic has also been the subject. As is well known, however, nonsubjects may be preposed, as in (201), and such sentences show the same sort of stress contour discussed earlier:[10]

(201) Now Jôhn I líke.

Such a sentence might be uttered by a speaker who is engaged in a discussion of different people found in a particular place. *John* is thus "old information" in the same sense as the topics in the previous examples were. It seems intuitively as if the rule of Topicalization reflects a preference for stating the topic first (a conjecture which seems quite plausible in view of the characterization of topics and comments that I have sketched above), though at the present time it is hard to evaluate the significance of such speculation. When the topic is not first, however, a distinct intonational pattern emerges— note (202):

(202) Now I líke Jóhn.

Both *like* and *John* in such an example are pronounced with a falling intonation contour; there is a distinct break between them.

The Topicalization facts just discussed contrast with the facts concerning Raising. Examples (203) and (204), as well as other examples in this section, indicate that topic-comment organization is possible in embedded clauses, as well as "news" organization, and both possibilities are retained in Raising sentences like those in (205)–(208):

(203) I expect that Jóhnson might dîe (or that something equally horrendous might happen).
(204) I expect that Trûman might díe.
(205) I expect Jóhnson to dîe.
(206) I expect Trûman to díe.
(207) Jóhnson seems to have dîed.
(208) Trûman seems to have díed.

thus suggesting that Raising is probably *not* sensitive to topic-comment organization. The passive "news" example in (209), which might be an answer to a question like (210):

(209) His dóg $\left\{ \begin{matrix} \text{was} \\ \text{got} \end{matrix} \right\}$ rûn ôver.
(210) What's wrong with John?

is also of interest in this context, since it has sometimes been suggested that the *raison d'être* of Passive is to provide a way of making the underlying object into a topic, as it were. While (209) argues against a sensitivity of Passive to topic-comment organization, in the sense that it shows that it would be wrong to claim that Passive can prepose only topics, it is worth noting that my earlier conjecture that initial position is a preferred position for topics might, to some extent, account for a greater acceptability of passive sentences at certain points within texts.

It is interesting to note that, of the three syntactic rules just discussed, Topicalization—by standard assumptions a postcyclic rule—appears to be sensitive to topic-comment organization, while the cyclic rules of Raising and Passive appear not to be. This finding is of some interest because it is in line with the recent hypothesis of Hankamer (1974) that only postcyclic rules can have what he refers to as "absolute discourse conditions." It should be obvious, however, that this finding can be taken only as suggestive, in view of the extremely small number of examples considered here, and that future research is required in this area as well.[11]

The examples discussed in this section, then, seem to point to an important difference in the organization of utterances: those utterances which are organized into a topic and comment receive a heavy stress on both the topic and the comment. When the topic precedes the comment there is no intonation break between the two, and thus, ultimately, the comment receives the most prominent stress of the sentence by principle (III).

A RHYTHM RULE

We saw in Chapter 1 that [231] contours are extremely general in English regardless of the constituent structure of the utterance. This suggests a fifth important stress-assignment principle: a rhythm rule (V) whereby the tertiary stress in such a contour is conditioned by the heavy stresses which flank it, rather than by any principle which refers to constituent structure. An additional conditioning factor seems to be the tempo of the utterance; thus, for example, (211) and (58) are both possible and seem to differ largely in that (211) is pronounced at a slightly slower tempo:

> (211) I lôoked ûp the ánswer.
> (58) I lôoked ùp the ánswer.

Similar pairs of examples can be given for the other types of cases discussed; a few examples follow:

> (212) côntext-sênsitive rúle
> (3) côntext-sènsitive rúle

> (213) bâdly-wrîtten páper
> (12) bâdly-wrìtten páper

(214) ôver-the-côunter sále
(5) ôver-the-còunter sále

The attentive reader will have noted that I have so far given no examples of topic-comment cases involving transitive verbs, where the
subject is the topic. Given what was said in the preceding section, we
should expect to find cases like (215):

(215) Jôhn hît Bíll.

Such cases do indeed seem to be perfectly possible, particularly if
there is a slight pause following *John*. We would expect, however,
that, at the right tempo, such sentences would undergo the same
rhythm rule discussed in this section; that is, we would expect that a
sentence like (1):

(1) Jôhn hìt Bíll.

is in fact ambiguous between a topic-comment sentence and a news
sentence. So far as I can tell, this prediction is correct.

The rhythm rule which seems to be operative in cases like these is
very much like principle (III), in that it refers crucially to the linear
position of items in surface structure and in that other principles are
logically prior to it. Unlike something like the NSR, however, neither
of these "surfacy" principles seems to depend on actual syntactic
structure in any way. Both rules depend rather on intonational conditioning factors and apply to the outputs of "deeper" principles
which do not refer to linear position of items in surface structure.

It must be borne in mind at this point that a precise statement of
this rhythm rule has yet to be given. My interest here has been in es-
tablishing that such a rule must exist in English; its precise nature is
beyond the scope of this work. An important aspect of this rule
which is of considerable interest, however, is its crucial dependence
on tempo—and, obviously, phrasing. A precise statement of the rule
must therefore await a useful theory of suprasegmentals; the rule is
clearly not statable in segmental terms.

In this chapter I have argued for the existence of four principles of stress assignment which seem to me to be well motivated and to be of great generality. Two of these principles refer crucially to the linear position of items in surface structure and "follow" two "deeper" principles which seem to have nothing to do with surface order. The former two principles seem primarily to be conditioned by suprasegmental factors, the latter two by factors relating to the discourse function of the items in the utterance. None of these principles refers directly to actual syntactic structure. Acceptance of the principles presented in this chapter thus entails a rejection of the *SPE* view that all rules relating to pronunciation form an interpretive component of the grammar.

6 Conclusions

SUMMARY

The position of Chomsky and Halle (1968) that the stress contours of utterances are assigned by cyclic rules which apply to syntactic surface structures has been shown to be incapable of accounting for most aspects of sentence-stress assignment. In this book five principles are presented which can be regarded as providing a first crack at accounting for sentence stress in a revealing way. These principles differ from one another in several fundamental ways and thus suggest that assigning the correct stress contours to sentences is not a matter of "interpreting" their surface structures.

The principle discussed in Chapter 4—that certain items in an utterance are treated as "insignificant" and not assigned stress—is a pragmatic principle which is unstatable in any current theory. Because of its great importance to stress assignment, however, it points to the pressing need for a theory of the relationships between formal properties of sentences and pragmatics; in the absence of such a theory we have no hope of giving a complete account of sentence stress. The need for such a theory can be denied only by denying that sentence stress is an aspect of our linguistic competence which we want our field to account for.

The remaining principles I have argued for in Chapter 5 are of different types. Two of these principles—(II) and (IV)—relate in some way to the discourse function of utterances rather than to (surface) syntactic structure directly. The two remaining principles, (III) and (V), which apply to the outputs of the others, relate to surface order of items and to suprasegmental factors (the division of the utterance into phonological phrases and the tempo of the utterance) but not to actual *structure*. These various principles seem, then, to relate to aspects of the utterance at different "levels" of the grammar. It can thus be said that a thorough understanding of sentence stress will come only with a thorough understanding of both pragmatic and suprasegmental aspects of utterances.

The fundamentally different character of the different principles argued for in this book argues against a basic claim of generative grammar: that stress-assignment rules are simply a proper subset of the set of rules that "interpret" surface structures by assigning them a pronunciation. It is not only not the case that such rules "interpret" surface structures—that is, that all and only syntactic structure at a level of representation after all syntactic rules have applied is relevant to stress assignment—but it is also the case that it is impossible to say that all stress-assignment rules are rules of a particular formal type. The existence of an interpretive phonological component of the grammar which is fundamental to such works as Chomsky 1965 and Chomsky and Halle 1968 cannot be maintained.

MORAL

While much of the acrimonious debate which has occurred in the last few years among linguists who had earlier accepted the framework of Chomsky 1965 has been concerned with empirical issues involving the nature of linguistic representations and the rules relating them, underlying this debate has been a fundamental split in the assumptions concerning how linguistic facts are to be studied. Thus, while linguists of the generative-semantics school have held that it is impossible to do "autonomous syntax," Chomsky has maintained a position which is represented well by the following passage:

> A central idea in much of structural linguistics was that the formal devices of language should be studied independently of their use. The earliest work in transformational-generative grammar took over a version of this thesis, as a working hypothesis. I think it has been a fruitful hypothesis. It seems that grammars contain a substructure of perfectly formal rules operating on phrase-markers in narrowly circumscribed ways. Not only are these rules independent of meaning or sound in their function, but it may also be that the choice of these devices by the language-learner (i.e., the choice of grammar on the basis of data) may be independent, to a significant extent, of conditions of meaning and use. If we could specify the extent precisely, the working hypothesis would become a true empirical hypothesis. Such an effort may be premature. It does, however, seem

noteworthy that the extensive studies of meaning and use that
have been undertaken in recent years have not—if the foregoing
analysis is correct—given any serious indication that questions
of meaning and use are involved in the functioning or choice of
grammars in ways beyond those considered in the earliest specu-
lations about these matters, say in Chomsky (1957). (Chomsky
1972:119)

   The stress principles which I have discussed in this book do not
obviously bear on the question of whether "grammars contain a substructure of perfectly formal rules operating on phrase-markers in
narrowly circumscribed ways," since the fact that they are not "independent of meaning or sound in their function" merely shows that
they are not part of the "substructure" to which Chomsky is alluding
—and, as he notes, his hypothesis is not formulated precisely enough
at this point to be empirically testable. It is my contention, however,
that the passage just quoted, like most of the debate in this area, con-
fuses two conceptually distinct issues. The question concerning a
"substructure of perfectly formal rules" is one concerning the formulation of a linguistic theory, an issue which belongs to the general
area of theory construction. Unless it is assumed that linguistic
theory is equivalent to a set of techniques for studying linguistic data
—an assumption rejected by Chomsky and most present-day linguists
—it does not follow that acceptance of a notion of a "substructure of
perfectly formal rules" entails the acceptance of the claim that "the
formal devices of language should be studied independently of their
use." The stress phenomena discussed in this book do have a bearing
on the viability of this latter claim.
   It is my thesis that it is precisely this view concerning the study of
linguistic data which has led to the false and, more frequently, empirically vacuous claims concerning stress which have been made in the
past and which I have discussed particularly in Chapters 3 and 4.
Knowledge of sentence-stress assignment is so undeniably a part of
our linguistic competence that no linguist has ever wished to suggest
that study of this area is outside of the scope of linguistics proper.
On the contrary, generative grammarians have held that the ability of
the theory to handle sentence stress in an elegant way is an outstand-

ing achievement of linguists working in this framework. As I have attempted to show in this book, however, this treatment is based on claims which are either false (for example, that the category membership of a given item is directly correlated with whether or not it is assigned stress) or vacuous (for example, that the heaviest stress in a particular syntactic constituent comes at the end except when it doesn't). Claims such as these are not the result of any failure to be observant enough; they are a direct result of an attempt to force sentence stress into a mold into which it will not fit. It is this very methodological assumption which has led to these false and vacuous claims.

Notes

Introduction

1. See Schmerling 1973 for further discussion of this problem.

2. This working definition of stress actually begs an important question, namely, that of whether some perceived prominences might better be attributed to intonational phenomena, rather than to stress. Liberman and Sag (1974) discuss one intonation contour containing a peak which they argue has mistakenly been taken by many to be a stress prominence. Following them, such a prominence can be considered a purely intonational prominence if (*a*) it is an integral part of a psychologically holistic melody and (*b*) the position of the peak is unrelated to word-level stress factors. By these criteria, the data discussed in this book are all examples of stress prominence, as the reader can verify.

3. See Lehiste 1970 for a good state-of-the-art summary of research in this area.

1. The Cyclic Approach

1. This is not to imply that the CR is without interest or problems of its own. See Schmerling 1971*b* for a discussion of this rule and a demonstration that the stress contours assigned compounds frequently cannot be predicted on the basis of surface structure (or anything else).

2. The structures indicated in this and other examples in this chapter are meant simply to be suggestive; all details not relevant to the present discussion are ignored. It should be noted in particular that, while the question of the proper labeling of the brackets in these examples is one over which there is some real controversy, there is general agreement on the bracketing itself and, presumably, on the distinction between lexical and phrasal categories which Chomsky and Halle's analysis assumes. I am aware of no disagreement in this area which might be relevant to the present discussion.

3. Chomsky, Halle, and Lukoff impose a condition on the use of junctures in a phonemic transcription, whereby a juncture may be used only at the location of a morpheme boundary. The actual use of a juncture, however, is for them motivated by phonological, not morphological or syntactic, considerations, so that the presence of a boundary does not necessarily entail the presence of a juncture in the phonemic transcription—nor is there a one-to-one correspondence between the type of juncture in the phonemic transcription and the type of boundary at a higher level of analysis, although they claim quite significant correlations between boundaries and junctures. It appears, then, that what discrepancies Chomsky, Halle, and Lukoff noted between boundaries and junctures in

the earlier framework have been translated into the need for readjustment rules in the current framework.

4. As indicated in the introduction, this is a rather perverse way of stating things. If surface structure is *defined* as that level of representation which is assigned a pronunciation, as it is "traditionally" in generative grammar, then the statement that stress contours are determined by the surface structure would appear to have the status of a tautology rather than an empirical claim. (There is an empirical claim lurking here, however, which is that there is *one* level of representation which is assigned a pronunciation.) Chomsky and Halle evidently have in mind a different characterization of surface structure: the output of the syntactic rules, where *syntactic rule* is defined not formally but in terms of motivation which can be found for positing the rule: syntactic rules must be "syntactically motivated." Since Chomsky and Halle argue for the existence of "readjustment rules" which alter constituent structure, the empirical claim they are really making is that "phonologically motivated" rules which alter constituent structure can all be ordered after "syntactically motivated" rules which do this. There are at least two respects in which their position is disturbing. First, their claims concerning a relationship between stress contours and syntax can hardly be said to have the significance they claim, since they apparently permit "readjustment rules" to alter the syntactic surface structure in any way necessary to enable the stress rules to give the right output; at the very least, quite heavy constraints on what readjustment rules could do would be necessary before their claims could be said to be of a testable nature (and it is obvious from their discussion that they do not intend readjustment rules only to alter constituent structure; the rules they propose do not form a unified class in terms of their formal properties). Second, it is doubtful that a clear-cut distinction between "syntactically motivated" and "phonologically motivated" rules that alter constituent structure can be maintained. In many cases there is abundant syntactic evidence for the existence of some such rule, but there is little if any "syntactic" evidence for the derived constituent structure which should be the output of the rule; see, for example, the discussion of Extraposition in Ross 1967. Syntacticians have frequently used suprasegmental facts as evidence for derived constituent structure, but a theory which permits "readjustment rules" renders any such arguments invalid.

5. Only the greatest stress in individual words is indicated, unless lower stresses are relevant to this discussion. It should be noted that [221] contours are generally possible for the examples under discussion as well; the difference between the two contours appears to be a function of tempo, as discussed in Chapter 5. Note that either contour is a problem for the cyclic approach, which predicts a [321] contour.

6. It may well be that in a thorough analysis these last cases are to be treated separately from the others, since they display fairly idiosyncratic behavior, while the other examples seem to be quite regular. [321] contours for (14)–(16) seem

quite possible, and speakers seem to vary a great deal as to which they use. In some cases there seem to be regional factors involved, as in *United States*, which I believe is limited to Southern speakers. Furthermore, cases which fit into the last group, if not to be considered compounds or idioms, are at least frequently used phrases which seem to have a special identity as such.

7. The existence of examples such as these is well known (see, for example, Jones 1960:253–254); the previous failure on the part of generative grammarians to recognize their implications for the cyclic analysis of stress is apparently due to a failure to recognize the fact that such expressions are widespread and, in fact, typical of English. Thus Bresnan is able to state: "There is a well-known case where internal stress relations are altered: compare the word *thirtéen* in isolation with the same word in prenominal position, *thìrteen mén*. If this were the general case, the cyclic principle would be unjustified; however, since it is exceptional, it is taken to be the result of some sort of special rhythm rule" (1972:333, n. 7). It should be obvious from the discussion here that Bresnan's example is not exceptional at all.

8. Such a rule would, of course, require information about constituent structure and thus is ruled out automatically if the notion of the phonological cycle formulated by Chomsky and Halle is maintained, since this involves erasing innermost brackets at the end of each cycle. It should be noted that examples like these point up a problem for another of Chomsky and Halle's rules, the Stress Adjustment Rule. This is the rule which lowers all nonprimary stresses within the word by one, and Chomsky and Halle collapse it with the NSR. Examples such as these indicate that this collapsing is impossible, since this rule cannot apply in just those cases where a patch-up rule would be necessitated. That is, we want to derive, for example, *Chámpaign-Urbàna, únknòwn quántity*, not **Chámpaign-Urbàna, *únknòwn quántity*, and thus the Stress Adjustment Rule, like our hypothetical patch-up rule, would have to apply on a higher cycle. I do not mean to question here the possibility that some rhythm rule is operative in these cases (see Ch. 5); I am simply discussing here a rule which would patch up the output of the NSR.

9. This statement is not quite right; actually, the rightmost conjoined constituent will have greater stress if it will thereby have the greatest stress of the sentence. See Chapter 5 for further discussion.

10. Bresnan (1972) does in fact propose such a rule, which she calls topical stress assignment.

11. Even an ad hoc remedy would deny that surface structure was the only level relevant to stress assignment, since it would require information about the derivational history of the NP.

12. Chomsky and Halle continue this discussion in a less than enlightening manner: "In connection with this problem, several comments are called for. First, it is very likely that certain readjustment rules . . . must be applied to surface structures before the application of phonological rules, deleting structure

and restricting the number of applications of the transformational cycle (and, consequently, the fineness of stress differentiation). Second, it is necessary to formulate a principle for interpretation of phonetic representations that nullifies distinctions that go beyond a certain degree of refinement. Third, there may very well be additional principles that modify the convention weakening stress when primary stress is placed in a complex construction."

I find each of these comments baffling. Readjustment rules could permit a [21] contour on *sad plight* in this sentence only if all internal structure were destroyed and, along with it, the cycle. Any principle restricting the fineness of stress differentiation would still be unable to produce a [21] contour on such a phrase, since stress levels lower than secondary must certainly be permitted. The third comment seems to contradict the general claims for the psychological reality of the cycle made elsewhere in *SPE*. (And, even disregarding this aspect of the problem, it is a serious question how such "additional principles" could be formulated. The problem appears analogous to that of how a grammar could itself be made to rule out sentences with too many self-embeddings.)

13. Bresnan 1972 contains a particularly clear discussion of this claim.

2. Other Approaches to Sentence Stress

1. Bresnan claims that a number of consequences concerning syntax follow from her ordering hypothesis—specifically, that deep structure in the sense of Chomsky 1965 exists, that the lexicalist hypothesis of Chomsky 1970*b* is correct, and that English is not a VSO language in the sense of McCawley 1970. As these arguments are outside the scope of this book, they will not be discussed here (but see Ch. 5, n. 2). They are criticized in Lakoff 1972 and Berman and Szamosi 1972; Bresnan replies to this criticism in Bresnan 1972.

2. C. L. Baker (personal communication, 1973) has pointed out to me that Bresnan can derive the correct stress contour in (60) without problems if Relative Clause Formation always applies to structures in which Particle Movement has applied. It is not obvious, however, how Bresnan could guarantee that Particle Movement applies in relative clauses. Note that her treatment of stress depends crucially on *look up* in this case having a full NP as direct object which is assigned primary stress at some point in the derivation. This is precisely the type of structure in which Particle Movement is normally optional.

3. Note that Lakoff's analysis refers to constituents which are direct objects in logical structure, and not, as his prose might suggest, to direct objects at a stage just prior to application of Question Formation or Relative Clause Formation.

4. Lakoff argues that a global rule of this sort is preferable to the ordering hypothesis of Bresnan on metatheoretical grounds alone, since, he argues, it

makes the stronger claim that no syntactic rule could ever depend crucially on the output of the stress rule. It is hard to see, however, how this statement holds. Lakoff seems to be saying that a global rule can "look back" in a derivation but not "look forward"—a claim which makes no sense in a theory like his, where a grammar consists of nondirectional "derivational constraints."

5. It should perhaps be pointed out that Lakoff's analysis differs from Bresnan's in a way which he apparently did not notice: the two differ in the total stress contours they assign even in those cases where they assign primary stress to the same constituent. In an example like *the girl John saw*, Bresnan's analysis predicts a [133] contour (or a [134] contour if the above-mentioned [221] → [231] rule is cyclic), while Lakoff's predicts a [132] contour—or would, if (b) were revised to give the results he intended. The derivations are shown below:

Bresnan-style derivation:

$[_{NP}$the girl $[_S[_{NP}$John$]_{NP}$ $[_{VP}[_V$saw$]_V$ $[_{NP}$the girl$]_{NP}]_{VP}]_S]_{NP}$

1	1	1	1	word stress
	2	2	1	NSR
			ϕ	Relative Clause Formation
1	3	3		NSR

Lakoff-style derivation:

$[_{NP}$the girl $[_S[_{NP}$John$]_{NP}$ $[_V$saw$]_V]_S]_{NP}$

1			(b)
	1	1	(c)
	2	1	(c)
1	3	2	(b)

6. This statement should probably be modified to read, "There is no systematic relationship between the structure of an utterance and all aspects of its
stress contour." Nothing Bolinger says concerning his examples is inconsistent
with the claim that certain aspects of sentence-stress assignment are directly correlated with certain aspects of structure—that is, he says nothing that would
argue against a claim like Newman's concerning the distribution of his nuclear
heavy variety of stress. In fact, in his discussion of an example which he tran-
scribes *I still have most of the gárden to wèed and fértilize*, Bolinger states, with
reference to the conjoined verbs, "We would predict—on a semantic theory—that
the more items are accumulated, the more apt they are to receive a main accent.
(WHICH ONE will get it—for example, *fertilize* rather than *weed*—may be a syntactic question, but that is not the point here)" (1972:635; Bolinger's emphasis).
Bolinger thus appears to be claiming that the "important" aspects of sentence
stress assignment have nothing directly to do with structure, but that matters of
phonetic detail very well may.

7. I have no alternative solution to offer to the problem presented by sentences (94)–(98) and simply note this problem for interested readers. I suspect
that a principled account of these cases must await a more general investigation
of sentences like these. Ladislav Zgusta has observed (personal communication,
1973) that a literal translation of (94) would not normally be used in Czech,
where one would simply say the equivalent of *John is wonderful*, and suggests
that English sentences like these may be typologically peculiar. A detailed investigation of the syntax of sentences like (98), with discussion of unsolved problems, is presented in Berman 1974.

3. The Normal-Stress Notion

1. It is almost made explicit in the following passages: "We assume that the
position of emphatic stress is marked in the surface structure, and we neglect
matters that we have assigned to the theory of performance" (Chomsky and
Halle 1968:25, n. 13). "I am assuming that the phonological component of the
grammar contains rules that assign an intonation contour in terms of surface
structure, along the lines discussed in Chomsky and Halle (1968). Special grammatical processes of a poorly understood sort may apply in the generation of
sentences, marking certain items (perhaps even syllables of lexical items) as bearing specific expressive or contrastive features that will shift the intonation center . . ." (Chomsky 1970*a*; reprinted in Steinberg and Jakobovits, eds. 1971:199,
n. b).

2. Bolinger (see Ch. 2) is one linguist to whom this statement may not apply.
If Bolinger's position is that the same (semantic) principles are relevant to stress

assignment in all sentences (which is not clear, since he does seem to be excluding from discussion certain examples which he considers "contrastive"), then he is, of course, arguing against such a dichotomy.

3. Later in their article, however, Berman and Szamosi note the difficulty involved in distinguishing between "normal" and "contrastive."

4. In order to reconcile the first sentence of this passage with what follows, one must assume that Chomsky is assuming that sentences which do not have "normal stress" or "normal intonation" are in some sense not entirely legitimate sentences.

5. There are other objections to this statement of Chomsky's. First, there is the trivial objection that *SPE* explicitly avoids any discussion of intonation. More seriously, despite his claims to the contrary, he cannot really be assuming a phonological component identical to that presented in *SPE*, since he argues for rules of semantic interpretation which refer to the output of the stress-assignment rules. Although he generally refers to this level as surface structure, he does admit that "it is, strictly speaking, not [the surface structure] that is subject to semantic interpretation but rather the structure determined by phonological interpretation of [the surface structure], with intonation center assigned" (p. 213). The key phrase here is "the structure determined by phonological interpretation of [the surface structure]." Since the *SPE* framework involves erasing innermost brackets at the end of each cycle, and since the stress-assignment rules are cyclic, in this framework the relevant level would have no structure. Thus, at the very least, Chomsky must be assuming a different characterization of the phonological cycle. If this level is the level of phonetic representation, then he is also assuming a different sort of phonetic representation.

6. Compare Berman and Szamosi's remark, "It is interesting to note that those of our acquaintances who are most inventive in concocting contexts in which 'semantically anomalous' sentences are acceptable found the widest diversity of possible stress patterns" (1972:314, n. 10).

7. I am grateful to Peter Cole for pointing this example out to me.

It has come to my attention that the pronunciation indicated in (113) is the "normal" pronunciation for a reply to a superior in certain segments of American society, such as the armed forces. This probably simply indicates that in such segments of society this phrase has acquired the status of a fixed expression even when used as a reply; note that a person who used (113) in this way would still not reply politely to a person named John as *Yês Jóhn.*

8. One might want to argue that we still need a notion like "normal relative to a given context" in order to account for utterances that are truly deviant. While I would not deny this, I am aware of no linguist's having used the term *normal* with reference to stress or intonation in this sense. Note that speaking of "normal stress" in this sense would be completely analogous to speaking of "normal syntactic structure" or "normal choice of lexical items."

4. The Question of Stressability

1. Again, it is hard to find explicit statements to this effect. Chomsky and Halle, in discussing the sentence (using their notation) $J\overset{3}{o}hn's\ bl\overset{2}{a}ckb\overset{5}{o}ard\ er\overset{4}{a}ser$ $was\ st\overset{1}{o}len$, state: "To prevent *was* from receiving primary stress by rule (2) [a tentative word-stress-assignment rule], we restrict this rule, as a first approximation, to the lexical categories, namely, noun, adjective, verb. We assume, on syntactic grounds, that the auxiliary *be* is not introduced as a member of a lexical category" (*SPE*, p. 22, n. 11). While it is far from clear from this discussion exactly what Chomsky and Halle mean by "lexical category," it seems safe to assume that they would not assign primary stress to nouns and to pronouns by the same rule(s). This assumption is maintained by Bresnan, who states, "I will assume that, by some means or other, anaphoric and indefinite elements are not assigned primary stress" (1971:258) and, further, "the NSR must 'know' whether it is applying to a pronoun or to a fully specified noun phrase" (1971: 271). Stockwell states, "Prepositions and Personal Pronouns (and . . . several other 'grammatical' or 'functional' classes, like Articles, some Auxiliaries, Modals, Conjunctions, certain classes of Particles and Adverbs—in general, all classes which can enter into satellite 'clitic' relationships with Nouns, Verbs, and Adjectives . . .) are obligatorily destressed (or never receive stress) and do not 'count,' as it were, in computation of the center of the NEUTRAL contour" (1971:26). These authors appear to differ in how they assume these supposed differences in stress assignment to be accounted for: Chomsky and Halle apparently assign responsibility to word-stress rules, Bresnan (and possibly Stockwell) to conditions on the NSR. The question does not appear to have been a major concern for any of these authors.

2. Chomsky (1970*a*), in his discussion of "surface-structure" semantic interpretation rules, seems to be moving closer to a position that recognizes a direct correlation between stress contour and "semantic" properties of sentences, though he clearly still accepts the essential correctness of the *SPE* view.

3. It is indeed difficult to give a noncircular interpretation to Trager and Smith's claim that syntactic constituents could be identified by their stress contour (or, in their terminology, by their superfix). On Trager and Smith's account, we can identify a constituent with a primary-secondary contour as a noun; if some other constituent has this contour the shift morpheme is present. However, the only way we can recognize the presence of the shift morpheme in some other type of constituent is by knowing that the constituent in question is *not* a noun.

4. It is not hard to see why statements that the significant correlation was between stressability and category membership might have been esthetically more satisfying than statements that it was between stressability and anaphoricity. A treatment of stress in anything like the "traditional" generative model would have to have involved stress rules which were sensitive to a feature like [± ana-

phoric] if the latter correlation was the correct one, and such a feature would be of a fundamentally different nature from features usually deemed to be necessary. Such a feature could not be an inherent feature of items like [±animate], nor could it be a transformationally introduced feature like [+ reflexive]; it would, rather, be a feature which was associated with items in *particular utterance-tokens* and therefore, in some sense, assigned by principles having to do with discourse. Thus the assignment of a feature such as this would have been something outside the scope of the theory, whereas category labels were something we could live with.

5. Newman identifies a "contrastive accent" which he characterizes semantically and which he states explicitly bears a nuclear heavy stress (see Ch. 1) which "can displace the nucleus of an intonational unit from its normal position on the final heavy stress to any word within the unit" (1946:177). Newman would thus claim that his "contrastive accents" are identifiable phonetically *in some cases*, namely, when they are followed by "subordinate heavy stresses" within the same "intonational unit."

6. Bolinger lists several relevant references in this passage.

7. Bolinger goes on to give several examples of intonation contours which have been called contrastive and argues that the same contours can appear in sentences which do not involve contrast.

8. It might be objected at this point that I have chosen a bad example "because *man* can mean 'person'." However, the feminist in me chose this example expressly because it can be shown that this commonly uttered claim is not supported at all by facts such as these. This can be seen by considering comparable utterances which involve different societal roles. Note (i) and (ii):

(i) We are looking for wŏmen who are interested in a career in núrsing.
(ii) We are looking for mén who are interested in a career in núrsing.

The description of the difference between (130) and (131) holds, *mutatis mutandis*, for this pair of examples as well. Now notice that an irate male could reply to (i) as in (iii) and get an embarrassed response like (iv):

(iii) What about mén who are interested in nursing?
(iv) Well, yes, of course—you know, it's interesting how so many men are getting interested in nursing these days.

But if an irate female replied analogously to (ii), a reply analogous to (iv) would be interpreted as a show of inconsistency on the part of the speaker.

The preceding does not bear on the use of *man* in sentences like (v):

(v) Man has always asked questions about the nature of language.

This *man*, which has all the syntactic properties of a proper noun, is apparently a distinct, though doubtless related, lexical item.

9. See, for example, Bresnan's claim cited in note 1 of this chapter.

10. As is well known, *any-* in examples like (137) and (138) appears to be distinct from the *any-* which appears in a sentence like *Ănyone could do that*. As the examples here show, however, the two *any*'s cannot be distinguished in terms of stress, contrary to the usual assumption seen in frequent statements concerning a "stressed *any*" and an "unstressed *any*." Not only can the *any* of the examples in the text appear either stressed or unstressed, but the *any* used in the example above may also appear unstressed in certain cases, such as *Ănybody with a bráin knows thát!*

11. A host of fascinating problems connected with these indefinite pronouns are unfortunately beyond the scope of this book. To mention one more, notice that the sentence *I've never seen ănything like thát before* seems to be paraphrasable by *I've never seen sŏmething like thát before*. On the other hand, a sentence like *I've never seen ánything like that before* cannot be paraphrased by **I've never seen sómething like that before*.

12. I have no explanation to offer for this fact.

13. Lakoff marks the stressed items in this example with acute accents; in changing one of these to a circumflex I am following the notational practice I have used elsewhere in this book. Nothing of theoretical significance hinges on this change, which is motivated purely for the sake of consistency.

14. Another case where significant differences in semantic relations may be crucial to stress assignment involves multiple WH questions, such as *Whô paid off whóm?* What is interesting about such a question for the present discussion is that the interrogative pronouns *must* be stressed: **Whŏ paid off whŏm?* is impossible, although interrogative pronouns generally may appear unstressed. As has often been observed (see Baker 1970, for example), such a question does not "question two different things"—it is not equivalent to a question like *Who was involved in paying people off, and who was involved in being paid off?* What such a question asks for is, in this case, a pairing of agents and recipients who were all involved in such activities, that is, a set of pairs of semantic relations. Thus such a question crucially involves contrasting semantic relations, in a way in which WH questions generally need not.

15. As Chomsky (1972) notes, Lakoff's characterization of the speaker assumption involved here is somewhat oversimplified. The characterization given in the text is accurate enough for our purposes here, however.

16. On the question of whether we want to talk about "semantic" presupposition, "pragmatic" presupposition, or both, see especially Thomason (forthcoming); Stalnaker (forthcoming); Karttunen (1973; 1974). The closely intertwined question of how presuppositions are to be represented has not received much attention in recent years; relatively early works on the subject such as Chomsky 1970a, Lakoff 1971a, and Morgan 1969b assumed that these should

be included in a "semantic representation" of a sentence, while Lakoff 1970*b* suggests a transderivational approach. A more recent discussion of this question within the framework of Montague grammar appears in Karttunen and Peters 1975.

17. Being quite naïve about questions concerning the distinction between stress and pitch when I wrote this earlier paper, I was unaware of the fact that the discrepancy between Chomsky's account of the facts and my own might be due to different conceptions of such entities. Despite the fact that Chomsky and Halle (1968) appear to have believed that stress was not physically definable, their references to stress and pitch indicate that they followed Trager and Smith in assuming that these were distinct entities; thus, Chomsky may, in the work under discussion, have been assuming different pitch "levels" in the sentences with different "foci" (though he nowhere states this). It is probably safe to assume that Trager and Smith, for example, would have maintained that the difference between the two versions of *John hit Bill* referred to in the text was purely one of pitch. As indicated in Chapter 1, however, this distinction between stress and pitch is at best dubious.

18. This problem is also noted in Lakoff 1971*a*.

19. This fact correlates in an interesting way with the fact that *telling* is not stressed in an example like *This is the dóctor I was telling you about.* As noted previously, this sentence might be used in a context where the presence of a doctor was in a sense remarkable. Thus the speaker can assume that the word *doctor* is (almost) sufficient to establish the identity of the person in question. Such an assumption could not be made by the speaker of (116). (This is not to imply that a sentence like *This is the dóctor I was télling you about* could not occur: such a stress contour does seem to be possible if the speaker assumes that *doctor* does *not* provide sufficient identification. It seems to me that a contour like this would most likely be used by a speaker who is frustrated by a show of apparent amnesia on the part of the addressee.)

It is worth noting in this context that Morgan (1973; 1975) has argued that this identifying function of restrictive relative clauses provides an explanation for why logicians have generally taken them to be presupposed true: in most cases this function is more efficiently served with a true description than with a false one.

20. A recent interesting discussion of these concepts is given by Chafe (1974), who attempts, among other things, to correlate them with pitch level. The material discussed in this chapter suggests, however, that such an attempt is misguided.

5. Relative Stress Levels

1. It is likely that some linguists have assumed some such notion as that of

"news sentence" to coincide with the notion of "sentence uttered with normal stress." There are at least two crucial ways, however, in which the two notions differ. First, as indicated in Chapter 3, it has generally been assumed that a "normal" stress contour is something which every sentence of the language has. I am assuming, on the contrary, that the meanings of some sentences are such that they would never be appropriate as news sentences; example (179) is such a sentence, as are examples like (99) and (100) in Chapter 3. Second, I am assuming that the notion of news sentence is one that is definable only with reference to the *function* of the sentence in discourse, and that there is no reason to assume the stress contours of such sentences to be in any sense "basic." In other words, news sentences are to be characterized as such on the basis of their communicative function; it is not necessary to adopt some notion of "neutral context" to define them.

2. There is one analysis which has been mentioned in the literature for which this statement holds only in part. This would be a combination of Bresnan's treatment of stress and McCawley's analysis of English as having VSO order throughout the cycle, with a postcyclic rule of subject formation. Bresnan (1971) attempts to show that the two analyses are incompatible, on the basis of the sentence *Jesus wept*, which she argues must have a [21] contour. If the NSR applied at the end of each cycle, as she suggests, and if at the point in a derivation where it would apply the sentence is represented as having predicate-initial order, then the NSR would assign primary stress to *Jesus*, reducing the stress on *wept*; thus, after subject formation, we would have a [12] contour. On the basis of the claim that this contour is incorrect, then, Bresnan argues that acceptance of her ordering hypothesis necessitates the rejection of McCawley's VSO analysis of English. If, however, one takes [12] contours to be the "normal" contours for such sentences with intransitive verbs, then, of course, Bresnan's and McCawley's analyses appear compatible, since they would together predict exactly this contour for such sentences. Such an approach would not, however, be as general as one would like, if the generalization under discussion is a linguistically significant one. This is because, in a sentence like (1), where we want both the subject and the direct object to receive greater stress than the verb, Bresnan's treatment will in fact assign primary stress only to the direct object. The greater stress on the subject would still be a result of something like her [221] → [231] rule, and the generalization that predicates receive lower stress than their arguments is still uncaptured.

3. This seems to be the approach of Stockwell (1971), in the passage cited in Chapter 4, note 1.

4. I label this evidence "slight" because proverbs are, of course, syntactically "frozen," and one might want to argue that their stress contours are likewise "frozen." It would be difficult to evaluate such an argument, since, as indicated in Chapter 3, fixed expressions tend to be stressed at the end, unlike this one.

An example of a proverb which is slightly more interesting in this regard, at any rate, is given in (i):

(i) One swallow does not a súmmer make.

The (slight) interest of this example lies in the fact that it is frequently used as a model for what might be termed nonce proverbs. A good example of this phenomenon, which I heard uttered during the recent streaking craze, is (ii):

(ii) One buttock does not a stréaker make.

5. In an analysis in which the verb-final order of (162) is transformationally derived from an SVO order, one might want to claim that the only difference between English and German stress was a rule-ordering difference: that rules of the sort which apply to surface structures in English apply in German as well but precede the Verb Final rule. This approach, however, still claims that there is a difference between English and German sentence stress which English speakers learning German will have to learn.

6. I base this assertion on my own experience and on the reports of two native speakers of German (Jürgen Döllein and Hans Henrich Hock) who have taught German to Americans.

7. Maling (1971), in an interesting study of stress-based alliteration patterns, argues for a similar tendency for verbs in Old English poetry to receive relatively lower stress. Such a tendency has often been noted for Germanic generally, which suggests that the principle I am arguing for here is quite old.

8. In what follows I will be using the term *predicate* as a convenient reference to either verbs or adjectives. The differences between adjectives and verbs, however they are to be treated in a grammar, do not seem to be relevant to the point at hand.

9. It will probably be objected by some at this point that the "vagueness" problem alluded to above renders principle (IV) useless. While the issue of terminological confusion is a real one, the fact that topic and comment are probably not definable within current linguistic theory does not, in my opinion, provide a valid argument against the approach I am taking here, as any theory must include certain undefined primitives; compare undefined syntactic notions like NP. The informal characterization of topic and comment that I have sketched here suggests that these notions are needed in a theory of discourse as well as a theory of sentences, and it may be that a useful theory of discourse can be constructed in which topic and comment can be defined in terms of more primitive notions.

10. I am excluding from discussion here the type of sentence in which only the preposed constituent is stressed. The term Topicalization has also been used for this type of sentence, which is characteristic of Yiddish English, but there are

a number of reasons for distinguishing the two types. They are used in quite different contexts, a fact which correlates with the prosodic differences between them, and, in addition, the type of sentence I am discussing here is not, to the best of my knowledge, limited to particular dialects of English.

11. There is another interesting contrast which has been observed in the literature which I suspect may be related to this area. Morgan (1969*a*) notes that a sentence like *He went home again* is ambiguous (at least as written) as to the understood "scope" of *again*, which may be *He went home* or simply *He be home*. (As Morgan notes, the same ambiguity occurs on a sublexical level in a sentence like *Open the door again*.) Examples such as these suggested to Morgan the existence of a rule relating an underlying structure in which the adverb is associated with a lower node in a tree with a derived structure in which this adverb is associated with a higher node. What is interesting about such cases for the present discussion is that, if *again* receives a primary stress in such a sentence, then its understood scope can only be the full sentence preceding it. McCawley (1973) attempts to account for this fact by imputing a destressing effect to Morgan's adverb-raising rule. I suspect that the stress facts here are, however, related to the general phenomenon discussed in this section. Notice that, if *again* in these examples is a "comment" and what precedes it—*He went home* or *Open the door*—the "topic," then the interpretation of these examples is correlated with the old-informationhood of topics. This suggestion is a necessarily vague one, but it deserves further study.

References

Akmajian, A., and R. Jackendoff. 1970. "Coreferentiality and Stress." *Linguistic Inquiry* 1:124-126.

Bach, E. 1968. "Nouns and Noun Phrases." In *Universals in Linguistic Theory*, edited by E. Bach and R. T. Harms, pp. 90-122. New York: Holt, Rinehart and Winston.

Baker, C. L. 1970. "Notes on the Description of English Questions: The Role of an Abstract Question Morpheme." *Foundations of Language* 6:197-219.

———. 1971. "Stress Level and Auxiliary Behavior in English." *Linguistic Inquiry* 2:167-181.

Berman, A. 1974. "Adjectives and Adjective Complement Constructions in English." Report number NSF-29, Department of Linguistics, Harvard University.

Berman, A., and M. Szamosi. 1972. "Observations on Sentential Stress." *Language* 48:304-325.

Bierwisch, M. 1966. "Regeln für die Intonation deutscher Sätze." *Studia Grammatica* 7:99-201.

———. 1968. "Two Critical Problems in Accent Rules." *Journal of Linguistics* 4:173-178.

Bolinger, D. L. 1958a. "Stress and Information." *American Speech* 33:5-20. Reprinted in Bolinger 1965, pp. 67-83.

———. 1958b. "A Theory of Pitch Accent in English." *Word* 14:109-149. Reprinted in Bolinger 1965, pp. 17-55.

———. 1961a. "Ambiguities in Pitch Accent." *Word* 17:309-317. Reprinted in Bolinger 1965, pp. 119-127.

———. 1961b. "Contrastive Accent and Contrastive Stress." *Language* 37:83-96. Reprinted in Bolinger 1965, pp. 101-117.

———. 1965. *Forms of English: Accent, Morpheme, Order*, edited by I. Abe and T. Kanekiyo. Cambridge: Harvard University Press.

———. 1972. "Accent Is Predictable (If You're a Mind-Reader)." *Language* 48:633-644.

Bresnan, J. W. 1971. "Sentence Stress and Syntactic Transformations." *Language* 47:257-280.

———. 1972. "Stress and Syntax: A Reply." *Language* 48:326-342.

Chafe, W. 1974. "Language and Consciousness." *Language* 50:111-133.

Chomsky, N. 1957. *Syntactic Structures*. The Hague: Mouton.

———. 1965. *Aspects of the Theory of Syntax*. Cambridge: MIT Press.

———. 1970a. "Deep Structure, Surface Structure, and Semantic Interpretation." In *Studies in General and Oriental Linguistics Presented to Shirô Hattori on the Occasion of His Sixtieth Birthday*, edited by R. Jakobson and S. Kawamoto, pp. 52-91. Tokyo: TEC Corporation for Language and

Education Research. Reprinted in Steinberg and Jakobovits, eds. 1971, pp. 183-216.

——. 1970*b*. "Remarks on Nominalization." In *Readings in English Transformational Grammar*, edited by R. A. Jacobs and P. S. Rosenbaum, pp. 184-221. Waltham, Mass.: Ginn.

——. 1972. "Some Empirical Issues in the Theory of Transformational Grammar." In *Goals of Linguistic Theory*, edited by S. Peters, pp. 63-130. Englewood Cliffs, N. J.: Prentice-Hall.

Chomsky, N., and M. Halle. 1968. *The Sound Pattern of English*. New York: Harper & Row.

Chomsky, N., M. Halle, and F. Lukoff. 1956. "On Accent and Juncture in English." In *For Roman Jakobson: Essays on the Occasion of His Sixtieth Birthday*, compiled by M. Halle, H. G. Lunt, H. McLean, and C. L. van Schooneveld, pp. 65-80. The Hague: Mouton.

Dougherty, R. C. 1969. "An Interpretive Theory of Pronominal Reference." *Foundations of Language* 5:488-519.

Green, G. M. 1968. "On *Too* and *Either*, and Not Just *Too* and *Either*, Either." In *Papers from the Fourth Regional Meeting, Chicago Linguistic Society*, edited by B. J. Darden, C.-J. N. Bailey, and A. Davison, pp. 22-39. Chicago: Department of Linguistics, University of Chicago.

——. 1973. "How to Get People to Do Things with Words: The Question of Whimperatives." In *Some New Directions in Linguistics*, edited by R. Shuy, pp. 51-81. Washington: Georgetown University Press.

Hankamer, J. 1974. "On the Non-Cyclic Nature of WH-Clefting." In LaGaly, Fox, and Bruck, eds. 1974, pp. 221-233.

Hill, A. A., ed. 1962*a*. *First Texas Conference on Problems of Linguistic Analysis in English*. Austin: University of Texas.

——. 1962*b*. *Second Texas Conference on Problems of Linguistic Analysis in English*. Austin: University of Texas.

Hultzén, L. S. 1956. "'The Poet Burns' Again." *American Speech* 31:195-201.

Jones, D. 1960. *An Outline of English Phonetics*. 9th ed. Cambridge: Heffer.

Karttunen, L. 1973. "Presuppositions of Compound Sentences." *Linguistic Inquiry* 4:169-193.

——. 1974. "Presupposition and Linguistic Context." *Theoretical Linguistics* 1:181-194.

Karttunen, L., and S. Peters. 1975. "Conventional Implicature in Montague Grammar." In *Proceedings of the First Annual Meeting of the Berkeley Linguistics Society*, edited by C. Cogen, H. Thompson, G. Thurgood, K. Whistler, and J. Wright, pp. 266-278. Berkeley: Berkeley Linguistics Society.

Katz, J. J., and J. A. Fodor. 1963. "The Structure of a Semantic Theory." *Language* 39:170-210. Reprinted in *The Structure of Language: Readings in the Philosophy of Language*, edited by J. A. Fodor and J. J. Katz, pp. 479-518. Englewood Cliffs, N. J.: Prentice-Hall, 1964.

Katz, J. J., and P. M. Postal. 1964. *An Integrated Theory of Linguistic Descriptions*. Cambridge: MIT Press.

Kiparsky, P., and C. Kiparsky. 1970. "Fact." In *Progress in Linguistics*, edited by M. Bierwisch and K. E. Heidolph, pp. 143-173. The Hague: Mouton. Reprinted in Steinberg and Jakobovits, eds. 1971, pp. 345-369.

LaGaly, M. W., R. A. Fox, and A. Bruck, eds. 1974. *Papers from the Tenth Regional Meeting, Chicago Linguistic Society*. Chicago: Chicago Linguistic Society.

Lakoff, G. 1968. "Pronouns and Reference." Unpublished. Distributed by Indiana University Linguistics Club, Bloomington.

———. 1970a. *Irregularity in Syntax*. New York: Holt, Rinehart, and Winston.

———. 1970b. "Linguistics and Natural Logic." *Synthese* 22:151-271.

———. 1971a. "On Generative Semantics." In Steinberg and Jakobovits, eds. 1971, pp. 232-296.

———. 1971b. "Presupposition and Relative Well-Formedness." In Steinberg and Jakobovits, eds. 1971, pp. 329-340.

———. 1972. "The Global Nature of the Nuclear Stress Rule." *Language* 48: 285-303.

Langendoen, D. T., and H. Savin. 1971. "The Projection Problem for Presuppositions." In *Studies in Linguistic Semantics*, edited by C. J. Fillmore and D. T. Langendoen, pp. 54-60. New York: Holt, Rinehart, and Winston.

Lehiste, I. 1970. *Suprasegmentals*. Cambridge: MIT Press.

Liberman, M., and I. Sag. 1974. "Prosodic Form and Discourse Function." In LaGaly, Fox, and Bruck, eds. 1974, pp. 416-427.

Lieberman, P. 1965. "On the Acoustic Basis of the Perception of Intonation by Linguists." *Word* 21:40-54.

McCawley, J. D. 1970. "English as a VSO Language." *Language* 46:286-299.

———. 1973. "Syntactic and Logical Arguments for Semantic Structures." In *Three Dimensions of Linguistic Theory*, edited by O. Fujimura, pp. 259-376. Tokyo: TEC Corporation for Language and Education Research.

Maling, J. M. 1971. "Sentence Stress in Old English." *Linguistic Inquiry* 2:379-399.

Morgan, J. L. 1969a. "On Arguing about Semantics." *Papers in Linguistics* 1:49-70.

———. 1969b. "On the Treatment of Presupposition in Transformational Grammar." In *Papers from the Fifth Regional Meeting, Chicago Linguistic Society*, edited by R. I. Binnick, A. Davison, G. M. Green, and J. L. Morgan, pp. 167-177. Chicago: Department of Linguistics, University of Chicago.

———. 1972. "Some Aspects of Relative Clauses in English and Albanian." In *The Chicago Which Hunt*, edited by P. M. Peranteau, J. N. Levi, and G. C. Phares, pp. 63-72. Chicago: Chicago Linguistic Society.

———. 1973. *Presupposition and the Representation of Meaning: Prolegomena*. Ph.D. dissertation, University of Chicago.

———. 1975. "Some Remarks on the Nature of Sentences." In *Papers from the Parasession on Functionalism*, edited by R. E. Grossman, L. J. San, and T. J. Vance, pp. 433-449. Chicago: Chicago Linguistic Society.

Murphy, J., A. Rogers, and R. Wall, eds. Forthcoming. *Papers from the Texas Conference on Performatives, Conversational Implicature, and Presupposition*. Arlington, Va.: Center for Applied Linguistics.

Newman, S. S. 1946. "On the Stress System of English." *Word* 2:171-187.

Pike, K. L. 1945. *The Intonation of American English*. University of Michigan Publications in Linguistics, vol. 1. Ann Arbor: University of Michigan.

———. 1947. "Grammatical Prerequisites to Phonemic Analysis." *Word* 3:155-172.

Pope, E. 1971. "Answers to Yes-No Questions." *Linguistic Inquiry* 2:69-82.

Postal, P. M. 1971. *Cross-Over Phenomena*. New York: Holt, Rinehart, and Winston.

———. 1972. "Some Further Limitations of Interpretive Theories of Anaphora." *Linguistic Inquiry* 3:349-371.

Postal, P. M., and J. R. Ross. 1970. "A Problem of Adverb Preposing." *Linguistic Inquiry* 1:145-146.

Ross, J. R. 1967. *Constraints on Variables in Syntax*. Ph.D. dissertation, MIT. Distributed by Indiana University Linguistics Club, Bloomington.

———. 1972. "The Category Squish: Endstation Hauptwort." In *Papers from the Eighth Regional Meeting, Chicago Linguistic Society*, edited by P. M. Peranteau, J. N. Levi, and G. C. Phares, pp. 316-328. Chicago: Chicago Linguistic Society.

Schiebe, T. 1970. "On a Global Derivational Constraint Involving Quantifiers in German." *Linguistic Inquiry* 1:351-357.

Schmerling, S. F. 1971a. "Presupposition and the Notion of Normal Stress." In *Papers from the Seventh Regional Meeting, Chicago Linguistic Society*, pp. 242-253. Chicago: Chicago Linguistic Society.

———. 1971b. "A Stress Mess." *Studies in the Linguistic Sciences* 1:52-66.

———. 1973. "Subjectless Sentences and the Notion of Surface Structure." In *Papers from the Ninth Regional Meeting, Chicago Linguistic Society*, edited by C. Corum, T. C. Smith-Stark, and A. Weiser, pp. 577-586. Chicago: Chicago Linguistic Society.

———. 1974. "A Re-examination of 'Normal Stress'." *Language* 50:66-73.

Smith, C. S. 1964. "Determiners and Relative Clauses in a Generative Grammar of English." *Language* 40:37-52. Reprinted in *Modern Studies in Eng-

lish, edited by D. A. Reibel and S. A. Schane, pp. 247-263. Englewood Cliffs, N. J.: Prentice-Hall, 1969.

SPE. See Chomsky and Halle 1968.

Stalnaker, R. Forthcoming. "Pragmatic Presuppositions." In Murphy, Rogers, and Wall, eds. forthcoming.

Steinberg, D., and L. Jakobovits, eds. 1971. *Semantics: An Interdisciplinary Reader in Philosophy, Linguistics, and Psychology*. Cambridge: Cambridge University Press.

Stockwell, R. P. 1971. "The Role of Intonation: Reconsiderations and Other Considerations." *UCLA Working Papers in Phonetics* 21:25-49.

Thomason, R. Forthcoming. "Semantics, Pragmatics, Conversation, and Presupposition." In Murphy, Rogers, and Wall, eds. forthcoming.

Trager, G. L., and H. L. Smith, Jr. 1951. *An Outline of English Structure*. Studies in Linguistics: Occasional Papers 3. Norman, Okla.: Battenburg Press.

Vanderslice, R., and P. Ladefoged. 1972. "Binary Suprasegmental Features and Transformational Word-Accentuation Rules." *Language* 48:819-838.

Index